People's Guide:
Cat Care

Series Editor • Jason Flynn

Copyright ©2005, F+W Publications, Inc.
All rights reserved. This book, or parts thereof, may not be
reproduced in any form without permission from the publisher;
exceptions are made for brief excerpts used in published reviews.

Published by
Adams Media, an F+W Publications Company
57 Littlefield Street
Avon, MA 02322
www.adamsmedia.com

ISBN: 1-59337-613-8

Contains portions of material adapted and abridged from *The Everything®
Cat Book* by Steve Duno, ©1997, F+W Publications. Additional material
provided by Barb Kary.

Printed in Canada.

J I H G F E D C B A

Library of Congress Cataloging-in-Publication Data
Flynn, Jason.
Cat care / Jason Flynn.
p. cm. -- (People's guide)
ISBN 1-59337-613-8
1. Cats. I. Title. II. Series.
SF447.F59 2005
636.8--dc22
2005020250

This publication is designed to provide accurate and authoritative information with regard to the subject matter covered. It is sold with the understanding that the publisher is not engaged in rendering legal, accounting, or other professional advice. If legal advice or other expert assistance is required, the services of a competent professional person should be sought.
—From a *Declaration of Principles* jointly adopted by a
Committee of the American Bar Association and
a Committee of Publishers and Associations

For bulk sales, contact your local Borders store and ask to speak to the
Corporate Sales Representative.

Table of Contents

Introduction v

PART 1   Choosing a Cat 1
CHAPTER 1   Why a Cat and Other
                      Questions to Consider 3
CHAPTER 2   Choosing the Right Type of Cat 13

PART 2   Basic Cat Care........................... 33
CHAPTER 3   Making Your Home Cat-Friendly 35
CHAPTER 4   Training Your Cat 53
CHAPTER 5   Day-to-Day Care........................ 69
CHAPTER 6   Bad Kitty: Problem Behaviors
                      and How to Correct Them 95

PART 3   Kitty Culture 117
CHAPTER 7   Show Cats 119
CHAPTER 8   Cat Psych 101.......................... 133

PART 4   Cat Health 149
CHAPTER 9   Cat First Aid........................... 151
CHAPTER 10   Health Care for Cats.................... 169

Index 183

Introduction

So, you're not one who believes that the title "Man's Best Friend" is reserved for the world's canines. Perhaps what draws you to a feline pet is their highly defined sense of self. Or maybe you just have wonderful memories of that kitten your parents got you when you were a kid and want to make sure that you do the best job you can now that it's your turn to purchase a new pet.

With our *People's Guide: Cat Care*, you'll be more than prepared for just about any cat-related issue that arises.

PART 1
CHOOSING A CAT

CHAPTER 1

Why a Cat and Other Questions to Consider

Why choose a cat over a dog, bird, turtle, rabbit, or guppy? What are the distinct advantages and rewards unique to cat stewardship? As for the turtle, rabbit, or guppy, well, what can we say? They are all fine pets, especially for children, but are all, quite frankly, rather boring. They don't interact with their owners on a very intimate level, and are at best mildly interesting to watch. Birds, of course, can be quite interactive and rewarding, but again, their intelligence and hardiness leave much to be desired in comparison to the abilities of dogs or cats, and they can't relate to humans the way other mammals can. Birds can also be extremely noisy; just ask any owner of a solitary cockatiel! So then, why choose a cat over humanity's "best friend"? For several reasons.

Reason #1: Cats Can Live Comfortably in Small, Indoor Spaces

If you do decide on a cat, you seem to be in good company; for the first time in United States' history, cat owners now outnumber dog owners. A major reason for this trend is the increasing urbanization of our population. More of us are living in city apartments, often too small to comfortably house a dog and not close enough to the grassy open areas that dogs so love to romp in (and, of course, eliminate in). City life is congested, hurried, and rather unpredictable, all conditions that do not lend well to dog ownership. Our two-income, "go get 'em" lifestyles these days do not cater all that well to the needs of the average dog, a pet that, if given a choice, would certainly prefer that we all go back to a more pastoral way of living.

When the United States' population was more rurally based, owning dogs made a lot of sense. Plenty of room existed for them to romp and roam and play on the farm or in a big fenced backyard. You could just open the back door, let them out, feed and water them, and play ball with them once a day. If they got dirty you could simply hose them off. Dog ownership under these conditions was less stressful for dogs and owners alike.

Things have, of course, changed dramatically. The majority of us now live in urban or suburban areas; many of us inhabit small one- or two-bedroom apartments that serve merely as way stations, brief rest stops in between long work days. Often we pet lovers are single, and spend ten to twelve hours per day away from home, dealing with bosses, deadlines, health clubs and rush-hour traffic. There are not many dogs who can reliably go twelve hours in an apartment without being taken out at least once or twice. It just is not fair to expect that of these animals. Though a few toy dog breeds can be taught to use a litter box, most dogs are just too darned big or messy to master it. Burying waste is not an instinctive canine behavior, anyway.

Apart from the elimination problem, dogs do not enjoy being all by themselves for great lengths of time. They are very social creatures, used to the time-honored pack dynamic, and will not be content to sit around all day sleeping, preening, or contemplating how gorgeous they are, as our feline friends often no doubt do. Dogs tend to go stir crazy after a while, and have been known to be extremely destructive as a result.

Apart from the physical damage bored dogs can wreak when left alone for hours, there is the tension they feel when, in their minds, they are "abandoned" by you each day for up to twelve hours. Some dogs, especially those that may have been rescued from shelters, become very stressed out when left alone by their pack leaders for extended periods of time. This can translate into poor health, including diarrhea and a multitude of skin disorders. Stressed dogs that are cooped up all day often nervously lick themselves for hours and develop lick sores, small areas on their bodies that become raw. This type of "displacement" behavior can also be seen in humans, as evidenced by those who chew their nails to shreds or pick at scabs. A lonely, stressed dog may also become extremely vocal about his or her plight; there is nothing like an incessantly baying beagle to get yourself evicted, let me tell you.

People who live in apartments and are gone for ten to twelve hours per day simply cannot purchase a puppy and expect it to stay all by itself during the day. It isn't a natural behavior for a puppy, and it is not at all fair to the little fur ball. Puppies need lots of interaction with people and other animals at this age, to develop confidence and the proper social skills. Plus, there is absolutely no way you will be able to properly housebreak a puppy if you aren't there to supervise at least once every hour or two during the first three to five months of the dog's life. You will end up with a pet that constantly soils your rug, and you won't ever be there to correct the behavior. You will just come home six hours after the transgression has occurred and lose your temper with the pup, who by that time has no idea what you are mad about. She will simply begin to think that you just always come home in a sour, antagonistic mood.

REASON #2: CATS ARE LESS COSTLY AND TIME-CONSUMING THAN DOGS

Dogs are high-maintenance animals. They must be taken out fairly often. They eat much more than cats. They crave and must receive regular attention from you, the leader of the pack. Regular exercise and play is a must. At least some level of obedience training is necessary, as is a fair amount of grooming for many breeds. In addition, numerous dog breeds (such as rottweilers, German shepherds, Australian cattle dogs, and mastiffs) can show aggression toward humans outside of their packs, particularly if the dog has not been properly socialized or trained (a real problem with latchkey dogs). Many dog owners end up spending hundreds of dollars trying to solve complicated behavioral problems in their beloved canines, keeping all of us animal behaviorists in the chips. Dogs can also get very dirty, and can really stink up a home, especially one with lots of carpeting.

Dogs simply require much more maintenance than cats, especially in today's crowded, increasingly urban world. Many people just do not have the time, energy, or money to take one on.

Reason #3: Cats Are a Snap to Housebreak

Cats seem to come equipped with the natural instinct to bury their waste in a litter box (an instinct reinforced by watching their mothers perform the task). Clean and good-smelling, cats are generally rather quiet (with some exceptions) and usually not too rambunctious or destructive (again with some exceptions). Cats are perfectly content to stay indoors if raised that way, and can easily tolerate being left alone for long periods. Remember that they are not pack-oriented, and are instinctively programmed to please and amuse themselves. They consequently suffer little from separation anxiety when their owners are away, unlike poor Fido.

Reason #4: Cats Need Little Exercise

Cats do not need to be as active as dogs. Usually content to sleep or stroll casually through your home, they do not need to be constantly walked or played with.

Reason #5: Cats Don't Need Much Training

Cats generally require less training than dogs, who must be taught rules and given restrictions in order to stay happy, well-behaved members of a family. Most cats behave well enough from the start, usually don't make messes, and basically mind their own business quite well.

Reason #6: Most Cats Need Less Grooming Than Dogs

Even for longhaired cats, grooming usually takes an owner less time than it does for a dog, and shorthaired cats need very little if any grooming. Don't forget that cats usually keep themselves quite clean. Can you say the same for your dog?

Reason #7: Cats Are Far Less Aggressive Than Dogs

Landlords tend to be tolerant of cat ownership by their tenants, which simply is not the case with dogs, not only because of the mess dogs can make, but also for liability reasons. No landlord wants to rent to a person who owns an aggressive, dangerous dog. Cats on average tend to show far less aggression or antisocial behavior toward humans than do dogs, and so are not much of a liability concern to landlords, who must now do business in a very litigious world.

Reason #8: Cats Are More Independent and Less Easily Manipulated than Dogs

One reason why cats seem so much less removed from the wilder state of nature than dogs do is that they have not undergone the intense level of domestication that dogs have. Because of their pack-oriented behavior, dogs are able to learn intricate tasks quite well; this has allowed humans to use them in a wide variety of ways, including herding, protection, hunting, tracking, and sport. Because of their easy adaptability to new behaviors, dogs have been genetically and behaviorally manipulated to suit particular tasks more than any other species of domestic animal. For example, the Great Pyrenees, a large herd-guarding dog, was purposely bred to have a thick protective coat to insulate against the cold and a large powerful body to intimidate would-be predators such as coyotes or wolves.

It is hard to believe that the Chihuahua and the Saint Bernard are the same species, but it is true, despite the latter's weighing as much as one hundred times more than the former. Consider that level of size diversity in humans; how many of us would want to car pool to work with a muscle-bound Goliath weighing in at over one thousand pounds and standing over twelve feet tall? The extreme diversity of dog breeds in the world, combined with the dog's long history of service to us, has helped create an animal that is much farther removed from the natural state than is the domestic cat. Ratting seems to be the only job that cats have been able to reliably help us out with; though a crucial service throughout recorded history, it is one that has required no instructions, special breeding, or cajoling on our part. Cats just like to hunt and kill rodents, period. They would do this even if we weren't in existence. In any event, cats certainly have not to date made good retrievers, herders, or rescue animals; this seems to have saved them from having their genes and their characters molded to the extreme, the way dogs have been.

So, thankfully (in the opinion of all cat aficionados), the cat's ancient instincts have for the most part been preserved, leaving them with their characteristic "attitudes." Some persons dislike this intensely, citing the cat as a parasitic creature, unlike the more symbiotic dog, who returns love and can perform useful functions during its lifetime.

Reason #9: Cats Require Less Emotional Energy Than Dogs

Dogs can often sap you of emotional energy, leaving you drained by the end of the day. Lots of dogs play the "feed me, love me, touch me, see me, help me, play with me" game day in and day out. It can get to you after a while, although they can't really help it. Most dog breeds (with the possible exception of sight hounds and dogs such as the saluki or the Afghan) need regular emotional input from their owners. They have got to engage in the subordinate/dominant behavior game on some level, or else go loopy in the process. Cats, of course, do not bother with all the silly posturing and control games. They are simply in control of their own lives, period. If they walk away from you, it is because, quite frankly, they have got better things to do. If they come to you, it is because they choose to be with you, period. No ulterior motives, no manipulative head games. Just two equals interacting (at least in the cat's mind).

Reason #10: Cats Are Much Quieter Than Dogs

Dogs bark. They have to; it's in their resume. Being more protective of the home than cats, dogs feel the need to warn the other pack members in the home of the approach of potential invaders like the poor mail carrier or the neighbor from down the street. If you live in an apartment and have a noisy dog, you stand a good chance of being evicted. Most cats, though, are very quiet, and almost never raise their voices loud enough to make a fuss with the neighbors.

All the above traits make cats much easier to keep as pets than dogs, especially in a small apartment. Single people working long hours most certainly would do better choosing a cat over a dog not only from a convenience standpoint, but also out of fairness to the dog. Keeping a dog in conditions that do not suit it is cruel. Why not get a cat, an animal that seems custom-made for the position?

Of course cats do have certain traits that some persons find a bit hard to swallow. Cats are generally less affectionate than dogs, or are at least less overt about it. They aren't eager to please people; it just doesn't make sense to them. Of course if your likes and theirs coincide, then everything is just fine. Cats tend not to be fond of being handled extensively, unlike dogs, who seem to thrive on touch. A cat can learn tricks, but won't learn them as quickly or effectively as a dog. Felines won't perform to please you; they need to have a major motivator, usually food, to entice them into action. They also must be in a cooperative mood. It is a "what's in it for me" attitude, a charming narcissism, if you will. Do not expect your little Siamese "Colette" to be catching Frisbees in her mouth any time soon, though. Also, do not expect your cat to adore young children, who tend to overhandle animals and chase and tease them for long periods. A cat is not a golden retriever, so if you have toddlers at home, you might want to consider a house, yard, and a playful, loving puppy. Lastly, do not expect cats to be appreciative of little things you do for them. They are haughty and lofty and pretty; it would be like expecting Bette Davis to thank you for lighting her cigarette or holding her door open. Come on, get a clue!

Though cats are less needy and social than dogs, they make excellent companions for those who can truly appreciate them. Cats are beautiful, graceful, compact, clean, sensitive, sleek, and beguiling. They possess a quiet, sinewy strength, a trait not seen in other pets. Cats show a great deal of curiosity, and can be very affectionate with persons they are familiar with, usually those who know not to force their attentions upon them, but instead instinctively know to wait for cats to come to them. When they do approach, they will brush against you, meow in your ear, gently paw your nose, or curl up in your lap, encouraging you to lightly stroke them while they purr contentedly in perfect bliss.

CHAPTER 2

Choosing the Right Type of Cat

So you've decided you want a pet, and that a cat would suit your lifestyle better than a dog. Perhaps you live alone in a small home and just don't have the time or space to care for a friendly but time-consuming pooch. That's fine. You have chosen to get a cat who will provide you with companionship yet not demand your constant attention—a pet that can amuse itself fairly well while you are gone, greet you affectionately when you return, and then settle down to do its own thing. So how do you go about finding this perfect pet?

The first choice you will need to consider is whether to adopt a mixed-breed cat from a shelter or private owner, or go the purebred route, choosing from one of the forty or so cat breeds currently recognized by the numerous national and international cat associations in existence today.

Some potential owners decide that they want to purchase a purebred kitten or cat. They have the money to spend (anywhere from one hundred to over a thousand dollars for some rare breeds), and feel that one or two particular breeds have exactly the physical and behavioral characteristics they are looking for in a cat. For instance, some may want a quiet, reserved cat; they can predict with reasonable certainty that a Persian or Himalayan will meet this requirement nicely. Another family, though, may want a more active, feisty cat; for them, purchasing a Siamese or Abyssinian will definitely ensure that this need is met. In other words, the potential owner can more closely predict just what kind of temperament and physical characteristics a cat will have by opting for a purebred cat.

For other people, the choice is equally simple; they just go down to the nearest shelter, choose a cute kitten, and take it home, without so much concern for its ultimate temperament or physique. Indeed, most cats in this country and in the world are mixed-breed "rescue" cats obtained for little or no money in this way. Purebred cats are definitely in the numerical minority everywhere that cats are popular. This differs from the situation with purebred dogs, which constitute about one-third to one-half of all dogs in this country, and about the same proportion in the rest of the world. Other differences are that dog breeds number in the hundreds worldwide and the size variation from breed to breed can also be dramatic—just compare a chihuahua and a Saint Bernard! Apart from the much smaller number of cat breeds, size varies much less in the domestic cat.

But if you want a cat and your heart isn't set on a mixed-breed or a purebred, what are the criteria for choosing between them? First let's discuss the ethics involved.

Every week in the United States thousands of cats are euthanized by shelters because there are simply many more of them than there are potential owners willing to give them homes. It is a tragedy of epic proportions, caused by the ignorance and irresponsibility of current cat owners who neglect to have their pets neutered.

The point is, there are many cats and kittens in shelters right now who will be euthanized this week if not adopted. These cats are no less smart than their purebred counterparts, are just as healthy (if not more so), and will be just as affectionate and fun to own. The ethical question begs asking: Can you choose a purebred cat, knowing that so many mixed-breed cats are so badly in need of homes?

The number of purebred cats and kittens sold each year is a minute fraction of the number of the mixed-breed cats euthanized in the same time period; every purebred will easily find a home, and none are in jeopardy of losing their lives, simply due to their low supply and high demand.

This decision is a tough one. However, the well-meaning potential owner should not be overly burdened with this dilemma. If every owner of a mixed-breed or purebred cat practiced responsible ownership, the overpopulation problem would not exist. So the question arises: Apart from the ethical dilemma, what are the differences between purebred and mixed-breed cats?

PRICE

The cost of a pet can affect your selection process. A mixed-breed cat or kitten from a private home, for example, can cost nothing. The owners will probably be grateful for you taking the little fuzz ball off their hands (and hopefully will go out and get their female spayed). If you go to a shelter, be prepared to spend $25 to $50 dollars, enough for the shelter to cover neutering and vaccination costs. They will probably provide you with advice as well. Overall, a good deal.

A purebred cat is a different story. You pay for what you get, it seems. Breeders are in business, after all, and must make a profit to remain successful. You also pay for the uniqueness of the breed; purebred cats are far more uncommon than mixed breeds, and certain breeds are downright hard to find. You always pay more for that which is in demand. The price of a purebred kitten or cat can run anywhere from $100 for an unregistered cat to well over $1000, depending on the breed. A registered American shorthair kitten, for example, might sell for $200, whereas a Sphynx kitten could run as high as $2000.

Once you have your cat, expect annual veterinary bills to approximate $100 per year for a checkup and vaccinations. Food and litter costs also add up, costing anywhere from $150 to $200 per year for both, total. Neutering your cat (something you need to do unless you intend to breed your animal, which is best left to the professionals) will cost anywhere from nothing to $75, depending on the cat's sex and where you go. You will incur all these expenses whether you buy a purebred or not, so if you're using cost to determine which type of cat to choose, it's really only the initial purchase price that you should consider.

Status

Having a rare, exotic-looking breed of cat can be a good way to impress dates or start a conversation. Other than that, all cats are equally lovable, be they mixed-breed or purebred.

Predictability of Appearance and Temperament

With a purebred kitten, what you see is pretty much what you will get. It has a very closely crafted set of genes, which, among other things, control the cat's appearance. A Havana Brown in Arkansas, for example, is going to look just like a Havana Brown in Peru. Before your purebred kitten grows up, you will know what it will look like fully grown.

A mixed-breed kitten is a different story. You do not really know, apart from its basic coat color, what you will end up with in a year. Will it have long legs and a skinny body, or short legs and a stocky, powerful body? You can only wait and find out.

The temperaments of purebred cats are also quite predictable, owing once again to the control exerted over each breed's genes. All Persians will be somewhat reserved, and all Siamese will be lively and vocal. Those are givens. With mixed breeds, though, it is a tossup. You just can't predict what that little shelter kitten's personality is going to be like, unless you get to observe at least one of the parents (usually an impossibility) or the siblings. It could be outgoing and friendly or reserved and timid. You can't tell until it grows up.

Health

Mixed breeds (whose purebred ancestors are at least three or four generations removed) have drawn their genes from a much larger gene pool than have purebred cats, and may therefore have somewhat less of a chance of developing anatomical, physiological, or behavioral abnormalities. Mixed breed cats generally have fewer musculoskeletal problems and stronger immune systems than do purebred cats. Most breeders do an admirable job, though, of weeding out undesirable traits from their stock, so the problem isn't as serious as some might make it out to be. First-generation mixed-breed cats from purebred parents, though, have little or no advantage over purebred cats.

Breeding Opportunities

The only other viable reason for choosing a purebred over a mixed-breed cat is if you have decided to become a breeder and need to begin acquiring breeding stock. Let me caution you: breeding cats (or any other species) is not an endeavor to be taken lightly. An expensive proposition, it is usually not very profitable. Most breeders do it out of love for their particular breed, barely covering their costs in doing so. Do not breed cats if your only motivation is to show your kids "the miracle of birth." If you want them to really learn something, take them to a shelter to see all the unwanted kittens.

Strays

Many of us have opened our doors in the morning on the way to work, only to be confronted by a beaten-up adolescent or adult cat meowing at us and rubbing up against our legs. We pet it, look for tags, and when we find none usually go inside and get a saucer of milk or some leftover chicken from last night's dinner. We give it to the poor wretch, then go off to work. When we get home that night the cat is there waiting for us, meowing its head off. For a few days we go through the same routine, giving the cat water and some food, petting it, then leaving it to fend for itself. After a few days, though, all but the most disciplined weaken; we take the cat into our homes, set up an appointment with the veterinarian (which can be very expensive with strays), name the bag of bones, and go on from there.

Strays often make great pets; they seem to be very appreciative and particularly loyal to the person who saved them. There are some problems that must be addressed, though, with regard to taking in strays.

Health Concerns with Strays

- Many strays are infected with diseases such as feline leukemia, feline immunodeficiency virus, and/or feline infectious peritonitis, all deadly viral contagions that can be spread from cat to cat via saliva through sharing food, biting, or even mutual grooming. These can be passed on to any cats you currently have at home.
- Most strays come loaded with internal and external parasites, including various types of worms, fleas, and ticks. These too can be passed on to your current cats or dogs.
- Strays can often have injuries received during fights with other strays or with dogs, including cuts, abscesses from bites, and broken or sprained limbs. They may also be suffering from ear infections, intestinal disorders, or eye problems.
- Strays have not usually been vaccinated against anything, and may be carrying the rabies virus, deadly to all mammals, including humans.

Behavioral Concerns with Strays

Most strays that have been out there for a while have gone through a lot of heartache. Owners have abandoned or abused them. Animals have attacked them. Cars have tried to run them over. Consequently they tend to be much less sociable, and will almost certainly be aggressive toward other pets you may have, at least at first.

Life on the streets has probably taught them some hard lessons, and made them less trusting. They develop a certain timidity out of the need to survive. Strays may therefore not be as open to being touched or held as would a cat you have raised yourself; they may try to scratch or bite those who get too chummy too fast. A family with children should therefore think twice before adopting a stray.

Many strays will want to have continued access to the outdoors, even though it is where they took all their lumps. It's what they know. If you accede to their cries of "let me out," they will run the risk of getting into more fights and of picking up viruses and parasites and bringing them home to your other pets. A stray may also refuse to use a litter box for a while, due to inexperience or lack of practice, or from having to exert dominance over other strays by leaving feces unburied. It may take some time to get them on track.

Age

Generally, strays are of adolescent or adult age. Adult cats do not learn as quickly as kittens. In fact, any adult cat, be it a stray or not, has well-established behavior that will be very hard to modify if unacceptable to you. Starting out with a kitten gives you a much better chance at shaping the animal's behavior to suit your desires.

These are the major concerns regarding the adoption of stray cats. Perhaps you will, too, you old softy. If not, consider at least bringing the stray into the nearest shelter or finding a home for it by other means, so that it can have a chance to be adopted by a willing, patient person.

The first place that you might want to check into is the local Humane Society animal shelter, or any of the town- or county-run shelters. These all run a considerate, efficient ship, and normally have an informed, polite staff present to help you choose a kitty, as well as answer any questions you may have regarding procedures, supplies you may need, proper environment for the cat, diet, or where to find a good vet. The county shelters and the Humane Society also normally offer some sort of pet counseling as well as workshops on proper pet ownership.

Numerous privately run shelters surely exist in your area; open up the Yellow Pages and look under "Animal Shelters." You should come up with at least two or three. Though not necessarily as well funded as the county or the Humane Society shelters, most of these do an admirable job of caring for their "rescue" animals with the money available, primarily donations and fees charged for animal adoptions.

Both private and public shelters usually provide you with low-cost neutering services (usually a mandatory condition of adoption). The neutering fee is included in the overall adoption fee. Many shelters will also provide you with some food and litter, and perhaps even a litter box and a toy or two.

Choosing a Cat from a Shelter

Most of you want to adopt a healthy cat. Who can blame you? So, let's discuss that first.

Age

Consider the cat's age. Do not take home one that is under eight weeks old; cats that have left their mothers and litters too soon may show profound fear aggression and antisocial behavior toward others for their entire life. Though adorable, a four-week-old cat is a risky adoption at best.

Health

Observe the cat's general health. The coat should be clean and relatively free of mats, and should have no missing patches or any kind of scabbing, which could point to parasitic infections or an allergic problem. The cat's eyes, ears, and nose should not be emitting any kind of discharge. Any cat that is sneezing or scratching incessantly should be passed over, as should one who seems dull, listless, or scrawny. Look for any signs of diarrhea in the animals' enclosure, and try to spot the cat with the problem by looking for dried feces around its anal area. Also, observe whether or not the cats are using their litter box. Choosing one that already has this skill down pat will save you a lot of aggravation at home! While handling the cats, feel free to examine each one closely. Look at each one's coat, skin, eyes, ears, anus, etc. Be aware of any discharge, skin problems, red eyes, or bloated bellies that could denote a worm infestation. Observe if the cat's ribs are sticking out. Check the entire body over for any skeletal problems such as malformed legs, paws, spine, or jaw. Even check the cat's teeth and gums. An eight-week-old should have a full set of milk teeth, and its gums should be pink.

Size

Pay attention to size (relative to age). Does one cat seem stockier and larger-boned than the others? Does another seem long-legged and thin? Determining what size a mixed-breed cat will ultimately be is very difficult but not totally impossible; if you are looking for a particular build of cat, it won't hurt to try to determine this at an early stage.

Sociability

Shelters normally keep kittens together; this will allow you to evaluate their sociability with each other and determine which ones are dominant, submissive, curious, timid, and confident. Consider a kitten only after you have seen it interacting with other kittens. Look for a kitten that seems to be at ease around others, and shows a relaxed yet inquisitive nature toward you. Ball up a sheet of paper and toss it in among the kittens; see who gets to it first, and what the general reaction of the group is. A kitten that wants to play and shows no concern is probably a good choice. Avoid selecting any kitten that shows fear of you or the other kittens; this type may wind up with an antisocial behavior problem later on. Any kitten that swats or hisses at you or the other kittens in unprovoked anger or fear should be avoided.

Try clapping, whistling, snapping your fingers, or jingling keys and observe the reactions of the kittens. Look for the ones that show interest, and avoid those who seem disinterested or frightened.

FINDING A MIXED-BREED CAT THROUGH THE CLASSIFIEDS

Pick up today's paper and turn to the "Classified/Pets" section. You will find a glut of animals up for sale or adoption, from cats and dogs to hamsters, ferrets, and snakes. The abundance of mixed-breed kittens found here is the result of many owners' still not getting the message regarding neutering their pets; they let their unneutered cats roam around outside and breed and those with females soon find themselves caring for five cats instead of one. Their irresponsibility may inadvertently aid you in connecting you with the right kitten, though, for several reasons. First, if you go to a private home to adopt or buy a kitten, you will get to see the mother and perhaps the entire litter (the father is usually some cavalier stud roaming the neighborhood, so it's not likely you will ever get to see him). It is a great advantage for you to see the temperament of the mother; if she is extremely timid and antisocial, you might want to consider passing up her kittens, who could easily have inherited her trait for this undesirable behavior. Of course, be aware that the mother will probably be a bit protective and guarded at first, especially if her kittens are only a few weeks old. Try choosing an ad that offers kittens in the seven- to eight-week-old range; by this time the mother will be attempting to distance herself physically and emotionally from her kittens, who in the wild are self-sufficient by the fourth month. If the mother seems confident, curious, and at ease in your presence, chances are her kittens may reflect that in their behavior later in life.

The ability to see the entire litter of kittens will give you the chance to compare and contrast them behaviorally, allowing you to choose the one which seems most confident, curious, and at ease with you. You should observe and test each available kitten using the methods discussed in the preceding section, the only difference being that instead of testing unrelated kittens in a shelter, you will be testing brothers and sisters in a private home. The kittens will all be similar physically, yet will each show a unique personality relative to the others. When testing unrelated kittens in a shelter, you may be seeing one kitten from one litter, two from another, etc., brought together for a very short period of time under often-stressful conditions. Kittens from the same litter have been with each other from birth and are therefore more at ease with themselves and their environment. You can get a truer feel for each's real temperament. And many of these kittens will still be with their mothers, unlike shelter kittens, who have probably been separated from their mothers at too young an age. In general, kittens from a private home will be less traumatized and more revealing in terms of personality, provided you see them when they are at least seven to eight weeks old.

Going to the home where the kittens were born allows you to see firsthand just what type of conditions they were raised under. If the place is a pigsty and the owners have twelve pregnant females roaming the property, you know it is time to shove off. If the place is clean and the owners are easygoing and kind to you and the animals, you can probably assume that the kittens are getting decent care and will be relatively healthy. With kittens at a shelter, you don't get to see any of this; the owners might have abused the kittens or just left them at the shelter doorstep.

There are disadvantages to adopting from a private home. First, the owner will not be providing you with free or low-cost neutering services. You will need to pick up the tab for that yourself, which can average anywhere from twenty to forty dollars. The kittens will also probably not have been vaccinated or wormed; you will have to get that done (costing you anywhere from fifteen to thirty dollars). In addition, private owners usually know little or nothing about illness or disease; their kittens might be infectious and a threat to your other pets at home. Most shelters, however, screen out sick kittens.

A private owner will not provide you with any pet counseling or advice, or provide you with food, litter, or a litter box. You will be pretty much on your own.

ONE OR TWO?

Though cats are by nature solitary and can amuse themselves quite well throughout the day, it might do you well to consider adopting two kittens instead of one, particularly if you live alone and are gone for a good part of the day. Cats that spend most of the day alone tend to get into things that shouldn't be any of their business. A bored cat may destroy house plants, rip apart sofas, become overly vocal, or even forget its litter box etiquette. Being alone too long can be stressful even for a cat; this stress can eventually result in poor health. Why not consider adopting two littermates instead of one kitten? The advantages are:

- They will amuse each other, preventing property destruction and separation anxiety (remember that kittens, unlike adult cats, are still fairly social creatures).
- They will learn to be much more sociable than kittens raised alone. This may make bringing future animals into the home easier.
- They will retain a vestige of kittenhood into adulthood, making them more playful and accepting of strangers.

Two mixed-breed kittens won't cost much more than one. Additional costs would be:

- One additional neutering
- Two cats to vaccinate instead of one
- More food (though cats really don't eat that much)
- Two litter boxes plus more litter
- More toys and an extra scratching post

Adopting an Adult Mixed-Breed Cat

Some of you may go to a shelter or private home looking for a kitten, but spot an adult cat that is just irresistible. Adopting an adult or adolescent cat can have its advantages.

- 🐾 The cat will be out of the "kooky kitty" phase, and will probably be acting more like a cat should act. It will therefore be much less destructive around the home.
- 🐾 An adult cat's personality is already formed, allowing you to know just what that cat is like temperamentally. A kitten, though, is still developing; you may not get a good read on its true personality until it is six to seven months old. Also, an adult cat is more likely to have been trained to use a litter box.
- 🐾 An adult cat is precisely the size it is going to be; there are no surprises. A kitten may turn out to be either petite and longhaired or a stocky shorthaired brute. You just can't tell.

There are disadvantages to adopting an adult cat, as well.

- 🐾 An adult cat has set behavior patterns that will be very hard to modify. If some of these behaviors are undesirable, you might get stuck with a cat that annoys more than it amuses.
- 🐾 An adult cat in a shelter is going to be much more stressed than a kitten, for two reasons. First, because it is an adult, it will not be happy about being around so many other cats and dogs, also present at most shelters. Remember that an adult cat is not by nature a very sociable creature.
- 🐾 An adult cat in a shelter was either lost, wild, or abandoned; this means it had a life that it was accustomed to but now

misses. Cats are creatures of habit, and when suddenly removed from what they are used to, become stressed and worried.

Because of these last two stress-creating problems, it may be hard for you to accurately determine what an adult shelter cat's true personality is like. Adopting one out of a private home is probably a better idea; you can get a better feel for its temperament when it is still in its relaxed home environment.

Adopting more than one adult cat is not a great idea, as they will be very territorial with each other and could end up fighting constantly. Exceptions to this would be two adults that have been together for a long time and enjoy each other's company, or two adult littermates that have been together since birth.

What Breed?

If you decide on the predictability and unique characteristics of a purebred cat (and are prepared to fork over the bucks for one), then your next step is to decide upon a breed that is just right for you.

Locating a Good Breeder

Once you decide on the right breed, you must then locate a reputable breeder. Let's first define just what that means.

Reputable breeders should:

1. Have their purebred cats properly registered with a reputable cat association such as the CFA (Cat Fanciers Association). The CFA will determine whether a breeder's information regarding his or her pedigrees is accurate, and will also (for a fee) add your kitty's name to its pedigree and send

you a registration certificate. If a breeder has not properly registered his or her cats and will not provide you with a pedigree, politely walk on.

2. Strictly abide by the "standard" for the breed. A standard consists of the physical characteristics of a breed that set it apart from all others. It is a breeder's job to maintain this standard in his or her stock. You should familiarize yourself with the standards of your favorite breeds; if a breeder's cats do not closely match these, move on. Careless or greedy breeders will sell kittens or cats that are bad representatives of the breed. A Persian with a kinked tail, for example, or a Manx with a slight build do not meet the standards of those breeds.

3. Allow you to examine their cats for certain basic structural faults, including:

    - Kinked tail
    - Severe underbite or overbite
    - Polydactyl (too many toes on a foot)
    - Pronounced limp, indicating hip, shoulder, spine or leg problems
    - Improper coat color or length for breed
    - Incorrect head shape for breed
    - Incorrect tail length for breed
    - Improper build for breed
    - Incorrect eye color for breed

Other things to be aware of when visiting a breeder:

- 🐾 Be as curious about you as you are about their cats. Dedicated breeders want to see their kittens go to people who are capable of caring for them. If a breeder seems to put you

through the wringer, be thankful; he or she is a dedicated professional who is looking for more than just a buyer. If a breeder wants to know nothing about you apart from the color of your money, walk on.
- Take great care in deciding what two cats to breed, rather than just putting any female in heat together with a willing male. Bad breeders will mate any two cats to make a buck.
- Keep cats in a top-notch, clean cattery. Any breeder who allows the cat's environment to become filthy or overcrowded shows a lack of concern and professionalism, and should be avoided.
- Socialize kittens with other cats and people from a very early age, and also handle the kittens from the first week on to ensure that they will be happy and confident with people. Any breeder that seems to have the kittens isolated from human contact (or claims that socializing at an early age is bad) should be avoided.
- Attend and compete in cat shows on a regular basis, to keep their skills on a competitive level with those of other breeders and to remain in touch with trends.

So, where do you find these wonderful, caring, altruistic cat breeders? Here are a numbers of ways in which you might locate some:

Clubs

Most cat breeds have a club or clubs all their own, dedicated to the betterment and discussion of their favorite breed. You can locate the club or clubs for your favorite breeds by contacting one of the well-known cat registries listed in the Resources section of *Cat Care Journal*. Any breed club should be more than happy to provide you with information on their breed and to give you a list of reputable breeders in your area.

Magazines

Newsstand publications such as *Cat Fancy* and *Cats* magazine always contain a great amount of breeder advertising. Reading these may help you locate a local breeder of good reputation.

Veterinarians

Your local vet knows a healthy cat when he or she sees one. Ask him or her for a recommendation/referral to a good breeder in the area, or for contact with a client who owns an outstanding representative of the breed you like. That owner might be kind enough to put you in touch with the cat's breeder.

Cat Shows

Good breeders attend and compete at local and national cat shows. After finding a list of local shows in a cat magazine, attend some and talk to the breeders present. Get a feel for their competence while observing their cats firsthand. See who wins in your favorite breed, and get their card!

Classified Ads

Good breeders as well as lousy ones advertise in the classifieds, so contact and visit a number of breeders before making any decisions.

Once you have identified several breeders of good reputation, make an appointment to visit their catteries. Look for cleanliness and professionalism. Observe the adult cats; are they timid and nervous or friendly and curious? Also, pay attention to your gut instincts regarding the breeder. Does he or she come off as trustworthy, open, and curious about you, or guarded and rude?

There are additional concerns when selecting a purebred kitten. Price will vary according to whether the cat is "show" quality or "pet" quality. All this means is that a kitten with features considered perfect for the breed has potential to be a cat-show champion, and will therefore be more expensive (perhaps by a factor of two), whereas a cat with too long a coat or too short a face will cost appreciably less, yet still be just as healthy and well-adjusted.

Show Quality versus Pet Quality

As discussed in the previous section, most breeders will have both "show" quality and "pet" quality cats up for sale to qualified buyers. The show-quality cats will cost more because they will be perfect examples of their breed. These animals could eventually be entered into competition, and possibly do quite well. The pet-quality cats, on the other hand, have some minor flaw in structure or appearance that would prevent them from doing well at a show; perhaps the coat is the wrong color or a bit too long or coarse, or the tail has a slight kink in it. They are just as healthy and well-adjusted as the show cats, however, and can make great pets, so the breeder offers them for sale at a substantially lower price. If you don't care about showing or breeding your cat, you should seriously consider purchasing a pet-quality cat, provided the "fault" is not severe or debilitating in any way. Any cat showing pronounced skeletal deformities, for instance, should definitely be passed over.

PART 2
BASIC CAT CARE

CHAPTER 3

Making Your Home Cat-Friendly

So you've found the right kitty, and it's adorable, and you want to take it right on home and love it. Congratulations! Hold up a minute, though. You can't bring it home just like that; there are all sorts of supplies you're going to need, and a number of preparations to be made before that little scamp comes barreling in.

The first thing to consider is allowing yourself and the kitten or cat to have a decent amount of time together to get acquainted and make your new pet feel at ease before you rush back to work and leave the little cutie all alone for the day—something it has yet to experience if it is under ten weeks of age. Even an adult cat will also need some quality time with you to bond and feel comfortable in its strange new surroundings.

Be Around

The best possible scenario would be to bring the kitten or cat home at the beginning of a vacation. A week or two together will really help the two of you bond. It will also give you a chance to work the kinks out of the system, so to speak. The cat has a chance to explore its new environment, and you get to observe it and begin to know it as an individual. Remember that each cat is unique and will have its own peculiar behaviors and habits that make it an individual. During this time it will also begin to learn the "do's and don'ts" of living with you. You do pay the rent after all (don't forget to remind your cat of that every day). Having a week or two to accomplish this "settling in" will be of great benefit to both of you.

If a week is not possible, try to at least have a three-day weekend coincide with the cat's arrival. If the cat is coming from a shelter, most of them will have late hours on a Friday, allowing you to pick up the cat after work and begin three solid days with it before trudging back to work on Tuesday. If you are getting your cat from a breeder, talk to him or her to see if it will be possible for you to pick the kitten up Friday evening. Breeders will usually be understanding about this, and will appreciate that you are thinking about the happiness of one of their kittens. If you are getting your cat from a private home, the owners should be more than happy to accommodate you as well.

Indoor or Outdoor?

Before bringing your cat home, you will have to decide if it is to have access to the outdoors or if will be purely an indoor pet. Decades ago, when we lived more pastoral lives, there weren't nearly as many dangers as there are now threatening an outdoor cat. Although aggressive dogs, parasites, and fights with other cats have always been with us, the outdoor cat population was once much lower and more widely dispersed. Rampant overbreeding was not nearly as pressing a problem as it is today and feline infectious diseases were not nearly as prevalent. Roads were less heavily traveled. Though still not as safe as being indoors, years ago outdoor living certainly wasn't the proclamation of an early death that is today.

The simplest way to significantly increase your cat's lifespan is to keep it inside your home. Most neighborhoods, particularly urban ones, are rife with feline dangers, diseases and death. Even rural areas that are relatively free from the dangers that a city brings still will have an outdoor cat population that often carries a legion of diseases and parasites. Today there are many more animals out there roaming around, fighting and spreading diseases that are much more widespread than they were only ten or fifteen years ago. Your cat could be bitten, infected, or killed by a dog, raccoon, or another cat defending its territory. Then there are all the dangers that we humans have created, namely cars, trucks, buses, poisons, guns, etc. Countless numbers of cats get killed each year because of the hectic, crazed environment we have engineered.

Keeping your cat indoors will also prevent it from preying on small wild creatures such as songbirds that wouldn't naturally have hordes of domestic cats running around trying to kill them. They have a hard enough time on their own without our pets upsetting the natural balance of things.

Outdoor cats live significantly shorter lives than their indoor counterparts. They suffer more injuries, become much less sociable with people and other animals, and find themselves visiting the veterinarian far more often then they should have to.

As long as you provide your cat with a stimulating home environment, it will have no need to go outdoors. Cats kept inside from kittenhood on usually develop no desire to go outside. And why should they? The home is their territory; outside is some other cat's. As long as you neuter your cat before it is of breeding age (definitely before six months), you won't have the problem of your cat wanting to go outside to mate and fight.

An adopted older cat who has been used to going outside will at first insist on having access to an open door. It will probably sit by a window and cry, or at least stare out all day wondering why it can't get at those starlings drinking out of a puddle across the street. It will try to scoot out of open doors, so be aware of that and inform family and friends to go in and out quickly, looking to see if the cat is underfoot.

Set Up Kitty's Area

Try to make your cat's new indoor environment as fun as possible, restrict its access to open doors and windows, and just wait it out. After four or five months it is likely to accept the new situation and claim the home as its new territory.

The next step to take before the cat comes home is making the home environment safe. Cats (especially kittens) are very curious creatures and will get into every accessible nook and cranny of your home, including the tops of appliances, cupboards, and pieces of furniture that no puppy or dog could ever dream of getting to. Here are some steps that you can take to safeguard your feline's new environment before it ever comes home:

- 🐾 Check all possible escape routes, making sure that the cat has no way of accessing the outdoors. If a new cat does get outside within the first few days, it won't yet have a clear sense of where "home" is, because it hasn't had the chance to establish that yet. It could be killed or taken by another cat lover.

- Install childproof locks on the cupboards and drawers, even on ones that contain no dangerous materials. You do not want the cat to ever learn how to open these, or get into something potentially toxic. You also do not want to come home to find the pantry open and flour, sugar, cereal, dry cat food, and a host of other foodstuffs strewn all around the home.
- Install baby guard plugs on all the unused electric sockets. A curious little paw could enter far enough in to get a fatal surprise.
- Try to minimize the number and availability of power cords and wires in the home. Kittens will play with and possibly gnaw on them, and in doing so may be shocked or killed. Put wires under carpets when possible, or tack them securely along moldings or under furniture. Out of sight, out of mind.
- Remove all potentially toxic chemicals from the cat's domain. Everyone has household cleaners, bleach, insecticides, drain cleaners, or solvents under their kitchen sinks; make sure you attach a secure baby guard to this cupboard to prevent your cat from poisoning itself.
- Do not assume that something stored high up is out of the cat's reach. Remember, you have got to think in three dimensions with a cat. New cat owners used to owning just dogs can be especially vulnerable to this mistake. Don't forget; cats can jump! Paint cans, motor oil, turpentine, antifreeze, and so on in a garage or workshop your cat may have access to must be stored away behind locked doors.

Every new pet needs a few essentials to live happily in the home. Before you bring your cat home, make sure you have all you need right on hand. The following is a list of items you will probably want to have around when kitty comes home:

Food

A good, nutritious food is essential for your cat; you should have it on hand when you bring the little (or big) tyke home. What constitutes nutritious? Talk to the breeder, shelter, or veterinarian; one or all of them should have an educated suggestion for you. The breeder may even give you a small supply of what the kitten has been eating. Kittens will need different food from adult cats; kittens have higher protein, mineral, fat, and vitamin requirements. Always have a good dry food on hand, and consider supplementing it with a good canned food. Foods available at a pet shop will be of higher quality than supermarket-brand foods.

Food and Water Dishes

Nothing fancy needed here; a four- to six-inch-diameter stainless steel or glass bowl for food and the same for water will do just fine. Some owners opt for an "extended feeder" type apparatus that meters either food or water down into a dish as the cat needs it; this comes in handy if you go away on vacation for a few days and can't find anyone to come in and feed the cat. This type of feeder is available in most pet shops. Consider placing the cat's dishes in a spot that is easy to clean and where there will be as few interruptions as possible. Cats can be finicky eaters; placing the food dish in a highly trafficked spot may prevent them from eating properly. A quiet corner in the kitchen is fine provided you are not cooking some masterful meal that has you flying around the room and smells really, really tempting.

Litter Box and Litter

Cats prefer to bury their waste. They are neat little devils. To take advantage of this instinct, you will need to supply your cat with a litter box filled with litter. The litter box should be made of a durable plastic so that it can be easily cleaned and will not absorb and retain odors from the cat's urine and feces. If you are bringing home a kitten, consider purchasing a box that is only two to three inches high, so that the little one can have easy access to it. Older cats will do better with a box that is four inches high or more, to prevent them from scattering litter all over the room. Covered litter boxes are also popular, and allow the cat some additional privacy, which is useful if there is more than one cat in the household. Most covered litter boxes have a removable top; consider keeping the top off at first until the cat begins using the box on a regular basis. Also, consider having more than one litter box in your home if you have more than one cat. This will help prevent arguments and the accidents that can follow. You don't want a line in front of the litter box, do you?

Litter works by absorbing and submerging a cat's feces and urine, thereby reducing the growth of odor-causing bacteria. The most convenient litters are the "clumping" type, designed to collect the cat's waste into small clumps that can be scooped out and discarded. This type of litter will be the handiest and most economical for you to use, because it allows you to keep uncontaminated litter in the box while removing only the clumped material. Try purchasing this type of litter first; most cats will do just fine with it. Litter box training and the problems associated with it will be discussed later.

Scratching Post

Cats scratch to shed worn claw coverings and to help visually mark their territories. Your cat will want to scratch something on a daily basis. To prevent your sofa or recliner from being the object of your cat's scratching passion, provide it with a nice, tall scratching post, one that is at least three feet high, four to six inches in diameter, and covered with carpet or some other textured material that will interest your cat. Some owners use a six-inch-wide log with the bark left on, screwed down to a square wooden base to keep it vertical. Others go whole hog and make or purchase a four- to six-foot-high "kitty condo" structure, a multileveled, carpet-covered playland that most cats love. Place the scratching post near where the cat sleeps or naps; cats prefer scratching right after waking up, much like the way we like to stretch.

Cat Bed

Many of you will want your cat to sleep with you, and that's fine. But for those of you who prefer not to share the bed, you may want to invest in some type of cat bed, something comfy and warm enough for the cat to want to curl up on. Check out the pet shops; get something that has a washable cover and is large enough for the cat to stretch out on. Don't spend too much, though; cats are finicky and often turn their noses up at beds of our design. They prefer to define what they consider a bed, e.g., yours, or a comfy chair. You don't want to get stuck with a $40 empty cat bed.

Toys

Your new cat will need plenty of stimulation in its new home to keep it busy while you are gone. Playing with your cat will also be important and fun; it is a way to bond, and at the same time develop coordination in your young feline friend.

Consider providing your cat with a good number of teaser toys, fake mice, small rubber balls, or crocheted balls with catnip inside. Try giving your cat a cardboard box or paper grocery bag; it will love to play hide and seek and go nuts for the crunchy sound of the paper. You can even try a wind-up toy that scoots around the floor on its own spring power but make sure it is nontoxic.

Check out the pet shops and bring home some interesting toys for your cat; they will keep it occupied during the day, and prevent the cat from destroying valuables that you don't want it to mess with.

Travel Crate

Having a plastic travel crate on hand can be very useful to the cat owner. It is a safe way of transporting a cat in a car. Most cats do not enjoy car rides because of all the hectic, uncontrollable activity going on around. Being loose in a car is like being in a fishbowl to a cat; it feels vulnerable, restrained, and powerless. Putting your cat in a travel crate for trips to the vet or to the cat sitter will keep it more relaxed and in control.

You should have a travel crate with you when you go to pick up the cat from the breeder, shelter, or private home. Most pet shops have good-quality, airline-approved travel crates for sale; make sure the crate is large enough for a full-grown cat, but small enough to fit beneath the seat of an airplane. Keep a comfy pad or blanket in it for warmth and security.

Grooming Supplies

Grooming is an important part of cat ownership, especially for those who have chosen a longhaired feline. Apart from keeping your cat looking good, grooming it from an early age will also help it grow accustomed to being handled, something that, though disliked by some cats, must be done regularly, especially when you need to check it for parasites or injury. You will need the items discussed in the following sections.

Brush

Regular brushing helps remove loose, dead hairs from the cat's coat, can reduce the occurrence of hairballs, and helps keep your home hair-free. Choose a soft, slicker-type brush for your shorthaired cat; it will get the job done and not feel harsh on the cat's skin. For a cat with long hair, choose a brush that more closely resembles one that a human with long hair might use. Your local pet shop will have a wide assortment.

Comb

Though combing is not necessary for a shorthaired cat, any longhaired cat will need to be combed out after being brushed. Combing removes mats and tangles, which, when not dealt with, can become irritating to the cat's skin, and may have to be cut out with scissors, ruining the look of your cat's coat. Consider getting both a wide-toothed comb and a fine-toothed comb. Use the wide comb first, then follow up with the narrow. Any pet shop will have what you need.

Nail Clippers

Cat claws grow just like our fingernails, and will occasionally need trimming. If left too long, they can unduly damage your furnishings and carpet, and even give you a scratch or two. If you start trimming its nails during kittenhood, your cat will tolerate it as well as it does being brushed (provided you don't cut too short). You can use "human" nail clippers, but consider purchasing a set specifically designed for cats.

Scissors

Some active longhaired cats will get mats in their hair, no matter how diligently you brush and comb them. If a mat cannot be combed out, it may need to be cut out with scissors. You probably already have a pair that will work; just don't use huge ones that could injure your cat while you are working on the mat.

Shampoo and Conditioner

Bathing your cat should not happen that often; they are clean little devils. You may need to bathe your kitty, however, if it gets into something particularly dirty or oily. If you decide to forego hiring a groomer and do it yourself, you will need to have a good cat shampoo and conditioner on hand. Do not use products for humans, as they will be irritating to your cat's skin. Check out the good old local pet shop.

FIRST-AID KIT

Most cats will get sick at one time or another, and some may injure themselves (though indoor cats rarely do so). Though your veterinarian is the person to deal with sickness or injury, you yourself can treat minor problems such as a thorn in a paw, colds, small cuts, bruises, abrasions, tick removal, slight sprains, and eye, ear, and mouth inspections. If your cat becomes seriously injured or ill, you might actually be able to save its life if a veterinarian is not available right away. Your feline first-aid kid should include:

- A rectal thermometer
- A small penlight
- Tweezers
- Syrup of ipecac
- Rubbing alcohol
- Disinfecting solution
- An antibacterial scrub
- A small blanket
- Gauze pads
- A roll of gauze
- Adhesive tape
- Cotton swabs
- Mineral oil
- A stethoscope

All of these should be available in your local pharmacy. (Note: Do not give your cat any aspirin at all! It is lethal to cats! Home medical care will be discussed later in the book.)

Collar with Proper Identification

Even if you keep your cat indoors all the time, it is still possible for a door or window to be left open accidentally, providing your feline explorer with an avenue to the outside world. To help get your kitty back, make sure it wears a collar with a clearly legible identification tag on it at all times. Consider purchasing an elastic or "breakaway" collar; either will prevent your cat from choking should the collar snag on something. Your pet shop will have what you need. Make sure that you introduce the collar to your cat early in its life, so that you don't encounter lots of resistance. Remember that cats get very set in their ways, and won't like the idea of wearing a collar if they haven't for many years. For the cat that doesn't seem to take to wearing a collar, try putting one on the cat at first for only a minute; during this time offer the cat its favorite treat or toy, keeping its attention off the collar for the allotted time. Each day repeat the exercise, lengthening the duration of time that the collar is worn.

Walking Harness and Leash

Yes, you read that correctly. If this is begun during kittenhood, most cats will take to it quite well. Consider waiting until your kitten is four to five months old before purchasing a special cat harness; by then your pet will be feeling safe and secure with you, and will be large enough to fit into an adjustable harness that can be used into its adulthood. The leash should be four to five feet long and made of the lightest, thinnest material possible. Your pet shop is really going to like you!

Conditions at Your Home on Arrival Day

Try to have your home as quiet as possible for the cat's arrival. Do not have the radio or television blaring, and do not have a wild party going on (dogs like to party; cats don't). Avoid bringing the cat home on a day that construction workers with jackhammers are thundering away right outside. Do not bring kitty home on the day that the gardeners are out in full force with their lawnmowers and annoying leaf blowers.

Introducing Your New Cat to Children

Talk to any children you may have well before the arrival of the cat and explain to them that this is not a dog, and should not be manhandled, teased, yelled at, pinched, pulled, or put in the toilet. An adult cat especially will not appreciate small, unpredictable children running around, teasing, and pulling at it. Teach your children to quietly and gently approach and pet the cat if it seems open to the attention. The children can even offer the cat a choice treat, or, if it seems willing, offer it a toy to play with, such as a fake mouse or a teaser toy on the end of a wand. If the cat seem tentative, just let it investigate its new home while you and your children watch passively. The goal here is to start the child/cat relationship off on the right foot; if the cat is frightened or mishandled on the first day, it will not forget it, and may never be open to contact with children again. Kittens will be more playful and open to contact, but remember that they are small and frail, and can be easily hurt or panicked.

Introducing Your New Cat to Other Pets in Your Home

It is a good idea to temporarily restrict any pets you currently have to a part of the home away from where the new cat will first be brought. They will be curious and probably concerned in a territorial sense; if allowed to get right into a new cat's face, they could frighten or hurt it. When you bring the cat home (in its nice new travel crate, ideally), carry it into a separate room, release it, and let it live there for a day or two. Provide it with food and a litter box and make it comfortable, but restrict it to this smaller area for now. Then let your other pets have access to the rest of the home again; they will smell the new animal and be very curious, but they won't be able to confront it directly.

Once all the resident animals have become accustomed to the new cat's smell (and vice versa), you can consider briefly introducing them for a duration of about ten or fifteen minutes, with the new cat safely in its travel crate. Repeat this procedure several times over the next few days, even placing the crate in the same room with the other animals while they are eating dinner. During this time, the new cat should be living in the restricted room, still separated from the others. Finally, when it seems that everyone is calm and accustomed to the presence of the "new kid," begin letting the animals interact for brief periods of time without the use of the crate. Supervise, but be careful; if they fight, you could get scratched or bitten. (Apart from the pain it causes, a cat bite or scratch can easily be infected.) Realize that at some point there will be some territorial conflicts between the residents and the new cat. They will need to work it out amongst themselves, and eventually should. During the brief initial interactions, have a large glass of water handy to douse the animals if they really get into it; that will normally break up most fights. Do not expect them to be best buddies for a while. They should begin to at least tolerate each other's presence after a few weeks, though.

Always consider your motivations with care if you plan to bring a cat into a home with a resident dog, even if that dog has had previous good experience with cats. Chances are that the cat has not had any exposure to dogs, and will be terrified and very hostile. A kitten will have a better chance of bonding with a cat-friendly dog, but it still can be risky. If the dog is a puppy now, or was raised from puppyhood with cats, then you have got a great chance of getting them to bond. Otherwise, don't push your luck. You could wind up with a badly hurt kitty. And, by all means do not get a new cat if you know the resident pets are aggressive to other animals!

What To Do If Your Kitten Cries the First Few Nights

You can expect that your new cat or kitten will be at first confused and lonely for its old surroundings. A kitten especially will miss its mother and its siblings. What can you do to comfort it? Several things, including:

- Keep the animal interested in its new environment by having toys and other curious objects around for it to play with and investigate. Often something as simple as a brown paper bag or a large cardboard box will amuse a kitten for hours.
- Supplying the kitten with as much attention as it is willing to take, to fill the void left by its siblings or "buddies." Handle the cat, and begin to brush it lightly while speaking to it in soft tones.
- Considering allowing the cat to sleep with you, or at least next to your bed on a bed of its own.
- Keeping a radio on while you are gone; tune it into a talk radio station, and keep the volume low. This will give the cat the feeling that it is not alone.
- Getting more than just one cat or kitten. Get two (preferably littermates), so that they can amuse each other while you are gone. This is the easiest way to keep a kitten happy, and to prevention destructive behavior stemming from boredom or loneliness.

Showing Your New Cat or Kitten Where Everything Is

You will need to show the new feline in your life just where all the necessities are located. The food and water dishes, which most owners usually locate in a low-traffic corner of the kitchen, should already have some food and water in them to get the cat's attention right off. Place the cat right down in front of them and let it dig in if it wants (though it might not at first, due to a slight case of the nerves).

Equally important is for you to show the cat where its litter box is located. Most owners place it in a laundry room or the bathroom that gets the least amount of use. Set the cat down right in the box, then scratch your fingers in it a few times (making sure that the litter is fresh, of course!). Even if your pet is just a ten-week-old kitten, it will almost certainly have already had some experience using a box, and should catch on quickly. Make sure that you leave the door to the room open so the cat has regular access to its litter box. The easiest way to create a house-soiling problem is to forget to leave that door open!

If you have chosen to purchase a bed for your new cat to sleep on, decide where to put it and show the cat where it is. Many cats take very quickly to a nice, soft cat bed, while others decide on some other spot to snooze (often they pick your own bed).

Setting a Basic Routine for Your Cat

Cats like routine. They depend on their environment's being predictable and safe, with no hidden surprises or unexpected trauma. To that end, try to set up a predictable, scheduled routine for your cat. Try to:

- ❧ Feed the cat at the same time each day, and in the same place.
- ❧ Groom your cat at the same time and place each day.
- ❧ Play with your cat at or close to the same time each day, perhaps when you come home from work or when you get up in the morning.
- ❧ Try to wake up and go to sleep at fairly predictable times.
- ❧ Stick to whatever rules you have set down for the cat. For instance, if you do not want it to go into the room with the four-thousand-dollar sofa in it, then never allow it access to that room. Be consistent; if you don't want the cat to jump up on people, then never let it jump up, not even once.

Those are some general guidelines regarding scheduling, but realize that your cat will need far less of this than will a dog. In fact, most felines will settle into their own schedule, one that will probably not clash with your own needs and desires. If this is the case, just go along with it.

CHAPTER 4

Training Your Cat

Once you have your new cat settled in at home, you will want to begin establishing some basic behavior patterns for it. You will both want to create an atmosphere of mutual trust and cooperation, and have as little friction as possible between you. As an owner, you should provide your cat with the essentials, including food, water, shelter, companionship, and privacy when needed (your cat will let you know when it wants to be alone, trust me). You need to also watch after your cat's health and provide it with adequate medical attention when needed. Finally, you should try to develop a bond with your cat, and be there for it when it wants your affection or help. In return, your cat gives you companionship, trust, and respect.

In order for your cat to gain your respect and admiration, it has to abide by your behavioral guidelines. It, however, won't just magically know what these guidelines are; you will have to teach it. Once these basic behaviors are in place, you and your kitty will better understand each other's role in your relationship; you will both learn to appreciate each other more fully.

Litter Box Training

Most cats have an instinctive desire to bury their waste, an instinct that has been reinforced by watching their mothers and littermates do so. By the time you bring your kitty home, it should already have the behavior down fairly well (a kitten separated from its mother and littermates before the age of seven or eight weeks might not have this behavior down pat, yet another reason for not taking a kitten home too early). Thank goodness for this tidy habit! Their burying of waste in a litter box is one of the key reasons why cats make such great, easy pets to maintain. No midnight walks in the rain! Nevertheless, you will need to show your new kitten or adult cat just where the litter box is located, perhaps even placing it into the box and encouraging it to paw at the litter. Adult cats will most likely have this mastered, but kittens may need some initial prodding at first. If necessary, actually dig into the litter yourself (make sure it's clean, of course!) with the kitten in the box, watching. It shouldn't take long for the little one to get the idea. Quietly praise your cat when it begins to use the box properly, but you don't need to make a habit out of being there in a pesty way each time the little one does its business.

In order to ensure that your cat uses its litter box regularly, you should abide by the following rules as closely as possible.

- Once you decide on a location for the litter box, be it a bathroom, hallway, garage, or bedroom, keep it there. Remember that cats are creatures of habit, and will become confused if you move the box, especially to a far-off spot. Doing so suddenly could induce the cat to have accidents, so avoid it at all cost. If you must move the litter box to another location, try purchasing a second identical box; fill it with the same brand of litter, then place it in the new location, while still keeping the old box right where it is. Bring the cat to the new box and encourage it to use it, then leave the rest to the cat. If it seems to be getting the idea and is using both boxes, try removing the old box after two weeks. This should work, though it is best to stick with a good thing and leave the box just where it is.

- Put the litter box in a quiet place where the cat is not going to be constantly bothered by humans or other animals. You expect a reasonable amount of privacy, and so does your cat. If you have a cat-friendly dog in the home, you may have to locate the litter box outside of the dog's domain, perhaps up on top of a counter, table, or piece of furniture. Or, you could prop open the door to the room just enough to allow access to the cat but not the dog (assuming the dog is larger). This is a matter of respect; you certainly wouldn't tolerate a wet-nosed pooch bugging you during such a private moment.

- If you have more than one cat and have opted for two or more litter boxes, try keeping them close to each other, and make at least one of them the covered type. The cats shouldn't mind, and it will be more convenient for you; no one wants to cart litter or litter boxes all over the place.

- A cat that is particularly timid or aloof may require a covered litter box placed in a very quiet area. By providing this, you will prevent future accidents and appease your cat's sense of vanity and privacy. Just make sure the cat knows where it is; it should do the rest.

- The most important advice you can remember is to keep the box clean! The most common reason for a cat not using its box is that it's too loaded up with waste. Remember that cats are very clean animals and will not want to frequent a messy litter box. You should scoop out waste from the box every day, perhaps twice per day if two cats are using one box. At least once each week, completely change the litter in each box, remembering to wash it out with mild soap and water before refilling it with litter. Following this advice will help ensure that your cat will stay on track with its toilet-training habits.

- Stick with the same brand of litter. Cats get used to the texture and odor; changing that suddenly can result in the animal's refusing to use its box at all, choosing to use your flower pots, closet, or dirty laundry instead. If for some reason you must change the brand of litter, do so very gradually, taking three to four weeks to complete the changeover. Trying to switch the cat over too quickly may result in mishaps.

Following these rules should result in your cat's developing and maintaining good toilet-training habits. Once you have accomplished this, you can breathe a great sigh of relief!

Name Recognition

Many cats do not know their names the way that dogs do. This isn't because cats are not smart enough; it's because owners often do not teach their cats to respond to a name the way they do with dogs. We all assume that saying "Fido, come" will bring the pooch romping over to us. This is usually the case; dogs are easily trained to come on command. Most cat owners, though, never call their cats over to them, and so don't get into the habit of prefacing that or any other request with the cat's name. Cats just do not hear their names all that often, and hardly ever get rewarded when they do.

You should teach your cat to recognize and respond to its name. It will expand your cat's intellect and strengthen the bond between you. In addition, it will set the tone for future training because it introduces to the cat the principle of conditioned response, or positive/negative reinforcement for a behavior. It is simple; while you have your cat in front of you or on your lap, pet it right after saying its name. Do this each time you pet it or give it a treat. If you practice this from the time the cat is young, eventually it will associate the sound of its name with something pleasant. It will perk up its ears and pay attention to you, knowing that something good is on its way.

Crate Training

Teaching your cat to spend time in a travel crate will be of great help during the times when you have to transport it in a car or airplane. Most cats do not do well being loose in a car; they get nervous, and can panic when confronted by all the unpredictable noise and chaos involved in driving around town. Taking your kitty in an airplane will require you to have it in a well-built, airline-approved plastic travel crate that will fit under the seat in front of you. There is no way you could have a panicked cat running around a packed 747.

The waiting room in the veterinarian's office is another place where you will want to have your kitty safely in a travel crate. Many vets do not segregate dog and cat patients in the waiting room; your little fur ball could find itself sitting next to Goliath the rottweiler, who may or may not decide to gobble up your pet in one bite. The crate will prevent panic, and may save you or someone else from getting badly scratched or bitten.

Start crate training when the cat is young. Simply pick it up, stroke it gently, then place it into the carrier and close the door. After a few minutes take the cat out and give it praise and a great treat, perhaps a bit of smelly tuna. Practice this regularly, increasing the time as you go along. Once you have worked up to fifteen minutes or so, put the cat in the crate, carry it out to the car and go for a little ride. Then return home, let the cat out, and give it a super treat and sincere praise.

Make sure that you practice crating and driving your cat at least once or twice each month, so that when you do need to take it somewhere, it won't be much of a struggle for either of you.

Socialization

One of the keys to successful ownership of a cat (or dog) is doing all that you can to ensure that your pet will be confident, calm, and friendly around strangers. There is nothing worse than having your cat hiss, scratch, or bite one of your guests, family members, or veterinarian, simply because that person tried to pet, examine, or move the little fur ball off the sofa.

Several factors determine an animal's level of sociability:

Species

Cats as a species are less sociable than dogs, and will not be as tolerant of strangers or as willing to be handled.

Genetics

Some cats will simply be genetically predisposed to be more timid and aloof than others. This is largely determined by the genetic makeup of the parents; if they are overly wary of strangers, chances are their offspring will be too. This trait can be somewhat modified through training, but cannot be eliminated.

Breed

Certain cat breeds will be more sociable than others. A Persian, for example, will be more aloof than will a Siamese.

Time Spent with Mother and Littermates

Cats who leave theirs mothers and littermates before the seventh or eighth week of life will have a much higher chance of being timid and antisocial. Those who spend the first eight or more weeks of life interacting with mother and siblings will be more confident and socially aware. Cats made timid by leaving the litter too soon are nearly impossible to rehabilitate.

Past Experiences

A cat or kitten who has been abused or neglected in the past will tend to be much less sociable than one who enjoyed good treatment from the start.

Though cats are by nature less sociable than dogs, a kitten that has spent the proper amount of time with its mother and littermates can grow up to be quite confident and interactive, even with those it hardly knows. The keys to accomplishing this are threefold:

- Ensure your kitten came from sound genetic bloodlines.
- Make sure it spent at least seven to eight weeks with its mother and littermates before being sold or adopted.
- Socialize your kitty as much as possible, beginning with the first week it comes home. Most competent breeders, in

fact, will make sure to handle their kittens from the second week on, every day, to really impart an affection for human touch.

- Once your kitten is settled into your home, you should begin having regular handling, petting and grooming sessions with it. Include playing with toys as well; kittens love play, and learn to trust their playmates (namely, you). Also, have friends come over (not all at once) and practice the same techniques. Include men, women, and responsible children, and have them avoid roughhousing or being loud. Otherwise, let them bond to the little tyke as completely as possible. The more people you can get your kitten to trust, the better.

If you have adopted a timid, fearful adult cat, do not prematurely try having your friends handle, pet or groom it; they may get bitten or badly scratched. Instead, simply have one person at a time visit the home for several hours, with the cat present. Have each person stick around long enough for a timid cat in hiding to slowly come out to investigate. Do not have your friends follow the cat or try to pick it up; just have them there, near you. Also, try having each person drop a particularly great treat near the cat each time he or she comes near. The cat will slowly begin to associate the presence of this ominous creature with food that it likes.

Do not expect an extremely fearful adult cat to become very sociable. The best you should hope for is the absence of aggression, and an acceptance (on the cat's part) that your friends are not out to hurt them.

Socializing your kitten with other animals is a different story. The single best way to get cats to interact peaceably is to raise them together from kittenhood. If you want your kitten to have company while you are gone, bring one of its littermates home, or another kitten of comparable age. They will bond through play and form their own sibling understanding as to who is dominant and who is submissive. If you bring a kitten into a home with an adult cat or cats, it is likely to have a hard time fitting in, and may take more than its share of lumps before being tolerated. Remember that adult cats are extremely territorial; your resident adult cat has claimed your home as its territory, and will not want to share it with some young upstart. If you do bring a kitten or cat home into another cat's domain, make sure you pay as much, if not more, attention to the resident cat, especially when the new boarder is around. The resident cat will slowly begin to realize that even though there's a new joker on the premises, it is getting petted, stroked, and played with more than when it was the only game in town. This will help minimize conflicts.

The same "camaraderie of siblings" rule applies to socializing your cat with dogs. It is easier if both are very young when brought together. Pups and kittens raised together from a young age often become great friends throughout life. If either is an adult at the time of them meeting, it rarely, if ever, works out, and can end disastrously, usually for the cat. An older dog who has had exposure to cats for its entire life, though, should have little problem adapting to a new kitten; just make sure that you are there to closely supervise the animals' interactions for the first month or two. Never leave a young kitten alone with a dog, however friendly the pooch might be. Even in play it could hurt or kill the small feline.

Building the Conditioned Response

During the first few months of ownership you should begin to teach your cat about positive reinforcement for desirable behaviors. This is easy; simply praise and reward the cat for proper behavior. If it doesn't put up a fuss about being groomed, pet and reward it with a treat. If it responds to its name, reward it. If it acts in a sociable manner with other animals and people, reward it. Most cat lovers feel either that cats cannot learn or else are above being taught. How elitist and boring! Cats are smart, and deserve to be mentally stimulated just as much as dogs or birds. No one is suggesting that you teach your cat to retrieve ducks from a pond; just reward your cat for acceptable behavior. You will expand its intellect and make your life a whole lot easier.

"Come"

It is easier to teach your cat to come to you than you might think! As discussed earlier, many of you have already done so inadvertently; many cats automatically race into the kitchen whenever they hear the sound of the can opener.

Why should you teach your cat to come to you? First, it is a simple behavior that, when mastered by the cat, stimulates its mind and strengthens its social bond with you and the other family members. Second, the "come" trick can be used as a distraction behavior; if you see your cat about to do something naughty such as dig into a flower pot, instead of yelling at it or squirting it with water, you can opt for calling it to you and rewarding it. The cat will forget about the mischief in favor of getting petted and fed. Here is how to teach it:

1. Keep your cat on a regular feeding schedule, as discussed earlier. This will create in it a well-defined hunger drive, the basis for teaching all tricks. Cats that free-feed will not be as inclined to come to you, unless they feel like doing so at the moment.

2. Obtain a toy "clicker" device in a novelty store. You can use a whistle instead, but the clicker seems to create a more sudden, percussive noise that really gets the cat's attention.
   3. For one month, whenever you put food in your cat's dish, click the clicker repeatedly until the cat comes. Pet it, say "good," then leave it alone to enjoy its meal. Do this religiously, at feeding time only.
   4. Try this right before dinnertime: Position yourself within a few feet of your cat. With a great treat in one hand (perhaps a piece of tuna, or meat baby food on a spoon) and the clicker in the other, begin clicking the clicker while holding out the treat. Your cat should come right over for the treat, provided it is hungry. Practice this once each day, while continuing to click at feeding. As the cat catches on, gradually increase your distance, until, after a few weeks, you can click from another room and have the cat come to you.

This behavior should always be rewarded with food; praise and petting alone will not be sufficient motivation for your cat to perform this (or any other) conditioned behavior. Still say "good," though, when giving the cat its food reward. Also, never overwork this or any other trick; stop when the cat has performed it perfectly one time. Remember that cats aren't collies; they get bored with repetition. (Note: never punish or scold a cat for not performing a trick behavior. The cat does not have to do this; it is just a neat way of increasing its repertoire of behaviors and keeping it amused. Also, punishing a cat almost always results in a major loss of trust. A cat cannot be forced to do anything. It does what it wants to do. The trick, therefore, is to convince it that the desired behavior is its idea, not yours).

WALKING ON A HARNESS AND LEASH

Letting your cat out on its own can be dangerous. It can get into fights, catch diseases and parasites, get taken by other people, or get hit by a car. You will incur higher vet bills, and the cat will live a shorter life overall.

Supervised excursions with you, with the cat securely on the end of a leash attached to a harness, could be the answer. There are some major caveats to teaching this behavior, however. They are:

1. The cat must begin this behavior when young. Few adult cats will tolerate wearing a harness and being on the end of a leash. Most will panic and hurt themselves, or you. Only teach this behavior to a young cat who has developed a good level of trust in you. Also, some cats will be too naturally timid or nervous to try this, even as kittens. If your cat is like this, do not force it to comply.
2. Patience is the watch word. If you rush into this, your cat will rebel. Take your time.
3. Never take your cat out on leash in a busy area with lots of pedestrian and car traffic, startling noises, dogs, or any other type of hectic, unpredictable behavior going on. Your cat might panic if it feels threatened, resulting in stress and possible injury. Only walk your cat in quiet, predictable areas, preferably a backyard or quiet residential street. Remember, the cat will cooperate only if it wants to do something.
4. If at any time the cat resists or panics, end the session. Never continue any behavior that upsets the cat.
5. Keep your cat's collar (with identification tag) on, in case it gets loose.

Here are the steps you will need to take to teach your cat to walk outside on a leash. Attach the leash to a harness instead of a collar; the cat won't be able to slip out of it if panicked. It also prevents the cat from feeling a pulling pressure on its neck, something that panics many cats.

1. When your kitten is fourteen to sixteen weeks old (or after it has had all of its mandatory vaccinations), purchase a cat-walking harness from a pet shop. Make sure it is adjustable, so you won't have to buy more than one to compensate for the cat's growth. At first, do not even try to fit it onto the cat. Keep it next to its food dish for a week, or treat it as one of the cat's toys, teasing the little fur ball with it, getting it to paw at it and feel at ease around it.

2. After your kitten becomes accustomed to seeing the harness, pick the kitty up and stroke it gently while sitting on the sofa. At some point, begin stroking the cat with the harness, just a few times, so that it gets used to the feel of it on its body. Do this for several days before moving on. Praise the cat and reward it with a treat after each of these sessions.

3. After reading the instructions for putting the harness on your kitten, gently do so during one of your stroking sessions. Take your time, and stop if the kitten gets too nervous. Do not tighten the harness at this stage; just have it on loosely. Reward your kitten with a treat. Consider using meat-flavored baby food on the end of a spoon; it will take the kitten a while to finish this, increasing the time that the harness is on. The whole idea is to desensitize the kitten to the harness. Get it to associate the harness with wonderful

food treats. If at any time the kitten objects or balks, remove the harness and end the session. Do not move on until the kitten is relaxed with wearing the harness. All this should occur in the quiet safety of your home.

4. Increase the time that the kitten wears the harness, up to about twenty minutes, or the time that an outside excursion might last.

5. Once your kitten can comfortably wear the harness indoors for twenty minutes, clip a light leash onto it and hold the end. Praise and reward the cat with food. Eventually, you should stand up and encourage the kitten to walk around on its own in the room. Use a toy to coax it if needed. Do not let go of the leash; if the kitten takes off running, the leash could get caught up on something and injure your little friend. At this stage, try to minimize the amount of tension the kitten feels from the leash; try to follow it around the room with the leash loose. Work on this for only a minute or two at first, but gradually increase the time.

6. While increasing the time on the leash, also gradually let the kitten experience a small amount of intermittent leash tension. Slowly increase this until some tension does not panic the kitten (make sure you are connected to the harness and not a collar!). Never pull hard on the leash, or yank the kitten around. You are not teaching the kitten to heel; it isn't a cocker spaniel. You just want it to accept the feel of the leash and harness so that it can safely go outside. Take at least a week to desensitize the kitten to leash tension.

7. Walk your kitten around the home once each day until it grows accustomed to it. Remember to regularly and liberally reward it during the procedure with its favorite food

reward. By this stage the kitten should be relaxed and confident. If at any point it seems to be worried or resistant, back off. It is only worth teaching if the kitten begins to enjoy it.

8. With the harness and leash on, carry the kitten out into a secluded, quiet yard, then let it investigate. Follow it around and keep leash tension to a minimum. Work this for a few minutes, reward it, then pick up the cat and return inside. Gradually increase the time spent outside, and see if you can eventually get the kitten to walk back into the home on its own.

9. If the kitten is confident, consider walking it on a quiet residential street for a few minutes. Let it explore, but avoid hectic or dangerous situations. Above all, avoid cars and dogs!! You do not need to go to this stage; feel free to stick to the yard.

10. Take your kitten out once each day. Do not ever force it and never let go of the leash! Always have plenty of treats with you, and offer them liberally throughout the procedure. Also avoid taking the kitten out during inclement weather, which might stress it out!

CHAPTER 5

Day-to-Day Care

The First Eight Months

A kitten up to the age of six or eight months should probably eat at least twice per day. A very young kitten (ten to eighteen weeks) might do better with three or even four meals per day. In order to meet a kitten's nutritional requirements, you will need to provide it with two to three times the amount of food (on a per-pound of body weight basis) than for an adult. The amount of protein needed is higher for a kitten as well. It is therefore important to select a food specifically designed for a kitten. You can discuss the different types of foods available with your veterinarian or breeder; any one that provides the growing kitten with the proper amounts of protein, vitamins, minerals, fats, and carbohydrates should work nicely.

You can choose between three types of commercially available foods.

Canned

Canned foods are normally highly nutritious and have a long shelf life. They are expensive, however, and tend to be about 70 percent water. If you decide on a supermarket or pet shop brand of canned food, make sure it has your vet's approval, and be prepared to spend twice as much as you would on dry food. Be prepared, also, to have to clean your cat's teeth on a fairly regular basis because of the soft, nonabrasive quality of canned food.

Dry

Dry food is by and large more economical than canned food. It has a long shelf life owing to its very low water content. It will also stay fresher longer in your cat's bowl than will canned food, making it a better choice if you tend to leave food out all day. Dry food will also help keep your cat's teeth cleaner due to its abrasive quality. If you choose to feed your kitten or cat a dry food, consider opting for the higher-quality pet shop brands in favor of the cheaper but less nutritious supermarket foods, which can have higher amounts of preservatives and ash, and lower amounts of essential nutrients such as fatty acids and taurine. As always, consult your vet when in doubt.

Semimoist

Semimoist foods are often used as an alternative to canned. They are lighter and easier to store, and very palatable to most cats. These foods tend to be on the expensive side, however, and often contain preservatives, artificial coloring, binders, and sugar. In addition, they do not help clean the cat's teeth.

Many owners decide to feed their cats dry food and supplement it daily with some canned food to increase the available amounts of protein and fatty acids. This is not only a less expensive alternative to a canned-only diet, but will ensure that a growing kitten gets ample protein into its system without developing tooth decay early on.

Again, whatever food you choose to feed your young feline, make sure that it is specifically designed for a kitten. Feeding adult cat food (or dog food) to a kitten can result in stunted growth as well as many other physiological problems.

Very often a breeder will give his or her clients a week's supply of whatever food the kitten had been eating at the cattery. If this is so, simply continue purchasing this same food for the kitten, provided it meets with your vet's approval.

Feeding the Adult Cat

Though adult cats require a high amount of protein in their diet compared to dogs or humans, they still need less than kittens. An adult cat that is fed food designed for a kitten may, over time, develop kidney or liver problems, so when your cat is between eight to ten months old, make sure to switch it over to an adult cat food that meets the approval of your vet. Consider feeding your adult cat twice per day at regular times. This will ensure that your cat develops a hunger drive, or "appetite," an important aid not only in maintaining health but in training as well. Vary the amount you feed according the cat's weight and level of activity; a lazy, relaxed animal is going to need less food than a hyperactive one. Get into the habit of weighing your cat once per month, to track any losses or gains. Ask your vet what an ideal weight for your cat would be, then try to keep as close to it as possible. To weigh your cat, simply pick it up, weigh both of you on a home scale, then weigh yourself and subtract this amount from the combined amount.

Overfeeding

Overfeeding can lead to an overweight cat, possibly resulting in a number of health problems, including diabetes, heart disease, respiratory stress, and structural injuries.

Feed your cat enough each day to maintain an ideal body weight, determined by your veterinarian. Don't let your cat get plump; you will be doing it a favor.

A cat is considered obese if it is 15 to 20 percent over its ideal body weight (determined by your vet). Normally a cat should have a thin layer of fat underneath the skin which should not prevent an owner from feeling the cat's ribs. The typical house cat should not weigh more than twelve to fifteen pounds, unless it belongs to one of the larger breeds

If your cat is obese, you should severely limit or completely eliminate its between-meal treats, and cut back about 20 percent on the cat's daily food intake. In addition, try to get the cat to play more frequently, or teach it to walk with you on a leash. You can also try feeding the cat a "senior" or reduced calorie food; this will allow it to continue eating the same volume of food while losing weight.

Feeding the Older Cat

As your cat ages, its metabolism will begin to slow down. If the cat continues to eat the same quantity of food when it is nine as it did when it was three, it will gain weight, something that can put undue stress on its body. Like the younger obese cat, the older cat may need to begin eating a lower-calorie "senior" food in order to maintain a healthy weight. Trying this approach rather than simply reducing the cat's daily volume of food will give the aging cat the illusion that it is indeed eating the same amount each day.

The number of pieces will remain constant, but the total calorie count won't.

Be sure to take your aging cat into the vet at least once per year, and continue to monitor its weight once per month. If you begin to see a steady weight gain, try the senior food and see what happens.

Also, be on the lookout for constipation in the older cat, caused by reduced motility in the intestines, decreased liver function, and an increasing inability to absorb nutrients. After you consult your vet about this problem, he or she may recommend the addition of more fiber to the cat's diet. Commercially available fiber supplements can be used, as can oat bran. The addition of one-half teaspoon of olive oil once each day can also help.

Free-Feeding versus Scheduled Feedings

To a cat, food is one of the only behavioral motivators. You won't be able to get your cat to do much for praise or out of loyalty; leave that to the dogs of the world. Using the expectation of a food reward, however, is an excellent way to get your cat to pay attention and perform some desired behavior. For instance, some cats will come running to the sound of a can opener, expecting it to open its favorite brands of food. This is a perfect example of a cat being motivated to perform a behavior for food. This cat, whether the owner realized it or not, had been expertly trained to "come" on command. You can teach your cat many interesting behaviors if you want to. All you have got to do first is instill a healthy hunger drive in it. A cat that gets hungry regularly and predictably can be motivated to do many clever things in exchange for a choice tidbit at the right time.

The way most owners feed their cats, however, works to reduce a cat's desire for food. Most owners leave food out for their cats all the time; this causes the cat to eat small amounts throughout the day instead of one or two scheduled meals. The cat is never really hungry, and will therefore not be too motivated to do anything for a food reward (this is the main reason why some cats can be finicky eaters). It makes sense if you think about it, and relate it to cat behavior in the wild. How many cheetahs eat whenever the mood suits them? Zero. They eat when they make a kill, which might be once a day or once a week. This creates a hunger drive, which in turn motivates the cat to hunt in earnest. If food was always there for the taking, we would have a lot of lazy, fat, unmotivated cheetahs on our hands.

Having a hunger drive and satisfying it is a natural way of life for a cat. Feed your cat at regular times during the day instead of leaving food out all the time. Your cat will anticipate the arrival of food at a specific time instead of lazily picking at its chow throughout the day. It will become less finicky, and will have a hunger drive that you can harness to teach or modify any of your pet's behaviors you choose. In addition, cats that pick all day tend to be overweight; owners, when they see an empty cat dish, usually fill it up. The cat ends up determining how much it gets, not you. Those who eat specified amounts at regular times have a better chance of being close to their proper weight.

Feed your cat twice per day at precise times, perhaps in the morning before you go to work, then in the evening when you come home. After doing so for only a few weeks, notice how much more attentive your cat becomes, especially at feeding time! Your cat will also eliminate on a much more predictable schedule.

Of course, you do not need to feed at specific times. You can free-feed your cat without any ill effects, provided it does not overeat.

You simply won't create a strong hunger drive in the cat, and it will be less responsive to any kind of training you might want to do.

I'm including grooming in this basic training section because cats do have to be taught to accept the level of handling necessary to maintain a healthy coat. Unlike dogs, who love touch at all times, a cat must be conditioned to accept regular handling from an early age. It is training, pure and simple.

Coat Care

You should train your kitten or cat to accept being brushed and combed and handled on a daily basis. Again, as with all new behaviors, cats learn best when young. You should start grooming your kitten as soon as it comes home. A necessary activity, grooming helps remove loose hairs from the cat's coat that might, if left undisturbed, contribute to the formation of hairballs in its stomach. Hairballs can result from the cat's habit of always licking itself clean. Though normally regurgitated or passed by the cat, they can sometimes cause intestinal blockages that necessitate veterinary assistance.

Begin brushing your kitten lightly each day, just for a minute or two. Soon it will become relatively desensitized to the procedure, and may even look forward to it if you talk quietly, praise it, and perhaps reward it with a treat at the end of the session. Longhaired breeds may not yet have their full-length coats in when they are this age, but the hair may be long enough to get a comb through, so try this, too. Realize that any longhaired breed will need much more coat care than a shorthaired breed, so be prepared to work on this daily. If you wait until your longhaired cat is six or seven months old before you begin a grooming regimen, you may find it very hard going. So start the habit early, when the kitten is just ten to twelve weeks old.

If grooming is not your forte, seriously consider a shorthaired breed, which will need brushing less frequently, and will not need combing at all.

Trimming Nails

You will need to periodically trim your cat's nails when they get too long. Excessively long nails can ruin furnishings and hurt you, so it is best to learn how to do this. Trimming a cat's nails is a procedure that really needs to be started when the cat is very young; having its feet handled is never a happy experience for a cat, because the feet are perhaps its most valuable asset. Cats run, climb, and protect themselves with their feet, and also use them as sensing devices. An adult cat will not like your messing with its feet, period. Instead, let a professional groomer do the work two or three times each year. That way, your cat will not direct its angst and wrath against you, and your relationship won't be compromised. Let the groomer be the martyr!

Kittens can be taught to tolerate having their nails trimmed, provided you never hurt them. Here is the procedure:

1. Every day for one month, while petting your kitten, briefly and gently handle each paw. Massage each between your thumb and forefinger, exposing the nails as you do. Gradually make brief, casual contact with each nail, then heartily praise the little one and reward it with a treat or a toy.
2. Once your kitten is thoroughly used to having its feet and nails rubbed and touched, begin lightly touching each nail with the clippers once or twice during the handling procedure. Do not trim anything yet. Just continue desensitizing the kitten to the metallic feel of the clippers on its sensitive

nails. Continue this for two weeks, and praise and reward the animal immediately afterward.

3. After your kitten has learned to accept having its nails touched with the clippers, try very casually to clip just one or two. This is important: do not take off more than a sixteenth of an inch of nail! At this stage, you are just getting the kitten used to the action itself, and are also learning how much pressure it takes to trim a kitten's nails. You have to get your skills and confidence up to par before attempting to cut all the nails. Always be conservative with how much you trim off; trimming off too much will cut into the quick, a visible blood vessel running down the center of each nail. Only the overgrown tip of each nail has no quick; this small segment, rarely over one-eighth of an inch long, is what should be trimmed. If you do cut the quick, you will cause the nail to bleed. You will also hurt the kitten, causing it to lose a great deal of trust in you. It will certainly not want you to handle its feet any time soon. So, at this stage, go slowly and build your confidence.

4. Once you and the kitten are comfortable with the trimming of one or two nails, go ahead and trim the nails on one entire paw. Remember, just take off the tip! Do one paw each day until all four are done. Doing all four in one session takes too long; your kitten will get fidgety and nervous. The trick is to trim the nails confidently and quickly before the little one really knows what's happening. After each session, praise and reward the little tyke. It might be a good idea to have some styptic powder or flour on hand; if you do cut to the quick, either one of these powders will quickly stop the bleeding if gently pressed into the nail tip.

If this nail-trimming procedure makes you nervous, don't do it. A nervous hand will make a mistake. Take your cat to a professional groomer instead, rather than running the risk of losing your cat's trust.

Cleaning Ears

You should train your cat to tolerate having its ears inspected and cleaned periodically. Indoor cats need this far less than outdoor cats, but all owners should be able to check their cat's ears anyway. As with brushing, combing, and nail trimming, your cat must learn to allow you to do this. An adult cat will tend to argue, so again, it is best to start this procedure when the cat is young.

1. While you are stroking the kitten's head, casually rub its ears, then gently rub your pinkie tip around the inside of the ear. Do this with both ears, then praise and reward. Continue this each time you have the little tyke on your lap. Do this for a week before moving on. Make sure you inspect the ears for dirt, wax buildup, and parasites.
2. While stroking the kitten's head and ears, gently touch the inside of each ear with a dry cotton swab, just for a few seconds. Praise and reward your pet afterward. Repeat this for several sessions.
3. Dip the swab in mineral oil and repeat step two, and this time extend the period of contact. Attempt to clean off any dirt or wax on the inside of each ear. Do not dilly-dally; be casual and quick. Then dry each ear off with the dry end of the swab. Praise the kitten and reward it with food. (Note: Never stick the swab down into the ear canal; simply clean

the visible outer areas. If you see dirt or wax deep inside the canal, take your kitty to the vet.)
4. Continue to inspect and handle the cat's ears at least once a week, even if they are clean, so that the procedure becomes accepted and ingrained into the cat's little head. If all is done properly and regularly, your cat will learn to trust your handling more and more. (Note: if your cat simply hates having its ears cleaned, do not force it to endure the procedure. Instead, see your vet when its ears must be cleaned. Also, see your vet if your cat's ears are continually dirty or if they have a discharge, as it could be a sign of infection.)

Care of Teeth and Gums

Over time, deposits of plaque can form on your cat's teeth, mostly on the molars and pre-molars. You can clean off deposits of plaque from your cat's teeth so that it will not lead to the formation of tartar, a harder substance that you cannot clean off. If left to build up over the years, these tartar deposits can result in gum disease and loss of teeth, not to mention bad breath. Once tartar buildup is significant, your vet will have to clean it off using an ultrasonic device, with the cat under general anesthesia.

Plaque is a substance that forms when matter left on the teeth after eating combines with saliva and bacteria. You can minimize plaque by feeding the cat a mostly dry-food diet, which has a more abrasive, tooth-scouring quality than does canned food, and by cleaning your cat's teeth on a monthly basis, removing any plaque that has formed. This involves training the cat to accept your probing in its mouth, a very personal procedure as far as most cats go. As with almost all training procedures, start young. Adult cats will probably just tell you where to put your cotton swabs, thank you very much.

Here is the procedure:

1. While the cat is still young, begin gently rubbing its gums and teeth with a finger while you pet and praise it. Be casual and confident, and do not let your rubbing last more then five or ten seconds at first. Gradually build up the length of time that you rub the kitten's gums and teeth until you are able to cover all of the cat's teeth and gums (getting all the way into the back might be difficult with your finger, so don't push it).
2. After the kitten is used to your finger, switch to a dry cotton swab and continue the procedure. The swab will allow you easier access to the molars. Remember to be brief, casual, and confident, and always praise and pet the kitten during and after. Give it a treat when you have finished. Continue this once each day for a few days before moving on.
3. Wet the swab with warm salt water and repeat the procedure. Continue this once each day for a few days before moving on. Make sure you use enough pressure to remove any loose food you encounter on the teeth or at the gum line. Praise and reward the kitten afterward.
4. You can, if you want, apply a bit of baking soda to the moistened swab, or purchase a feline toothpaste from your pet shop or vet. Either will provide a slight abrasive quality that will help clean the teeth.

Look for chipped or loose teeth during the brushing. Also examine the gums for inflammation or bleeding. If you see any of this, see your vet.

Things to Look for in Choosing a Vet

Convenient Location and Hours

No one wants to drive their sick or injured kitty to a vet's office that is forty-five minutes from home. That ride could be potentially life-threatening to your cat. You should be able to locate a capable vet within ten or fifteen minutes of your home. Make sure that vet's hours are also convenient for you; see if there are at least a few days during the week with evening hours allowing you to take your cat in for a checkup after you get home from work.

Emergency Care

Emergencies never happen at convenient times of the day. Your vet should therefore provide convenient, efficient emergency care to his or her clients, or at least be able to refer you to a nearby emergency clinic when necessary.

Reasonably Priced

Though cost is not always on devoted pet-lovers' minds when their little friend is sick or injured, it nevertheless is an issue, particularly with regard to vaccinations, checkups, and neutering. Don't let this be your only criterion, but let it factor into the decision-making process. Also, beware of high-volume vet clinics that seem too cheap to be true.

Organization

The vet's office should appear well-organized and professionally run. There should not be irate clients walking around, dogs and cats fighting, or obviously sick animals waiting endlessly in the waiting room, possibly infecting other animals. The staff should be efficient and polite, and your appointment time should be honored within reason. Avoid vet clinics that seem chaotic, rude, and disorganized. The clinic should always be clean and orderly.

Communication

Stick with a vet that seems easy to talk to and willing to listen. A vet needs to be as good with people as he or she is with animals, and be able to explain things succinctly and compassionately without getting overly technical. Avoid a vet who seems rushed, impolite, or put off by reasonable questions. Choose someone who seems knowledgeable, kind, and genuinely interested in the health of your pet. If you don't feel at ease with the vet, find another that is more personable.

Participation

Choose a vet who allows you to be present during your pet's examination. You can learn a lot about your pet and your vet by observing the exam. Do not expect to be present for surgeries or any emergency procedures, however; you will just get in the way.

Knowledge

Stick with a vet who keeps up with the most current medical information and tries to improve his or her skills through continuing education and training. Beware of vets who "swear by the old ways."

You should take your new kitten or cat in to the veterinary clinic within a week of its coming home. You need to determine the cat's general state of health, ensure that there are no infectious diseases present, get it properly vaccinated, and start the vet/pet relationship.

Now that you know what you're looking for, how do you find this wonderful, kind animal doctor? There are four basic ways:

Reference from a Friend or Relative

A much better method than throwing a dart at the Yellow Pages is asking friends or relatives if they are happy with their vet. The fact that someone has stuck with a vet for a period of time is a good sign. Consider trying this vet out; if you aren't pleased, just find another.

Recommendation from the Shelter or Breeder

The shelter from which you adopt your cat can probably recommend one or two reputable vets in your area. Shelters deal with hundreds of animals and often have sick ones in need of medical attention. Their on-call vet just might be the most experienced cat vet in the area, so consider a shelter recommendation seriously. If you purchased your cat from a breeder, he or she can definitely recommend a good vet, possibly the one he or she uses. One drawback to this method is that your breeder might not be located near your home, and won't know a vet that will be convenient for you. Ask anyway; the breeder just might know someone in your area, or his or her vet might be able to recommend someone close to you.

You can take a direct role in preventing many disorders from seriously affecting your cat simply by taking precautions, and by being properly prepared for sickness or injury if and when they do occur. As a cat owner, you have an almost parental responsibility to provide your cat with the most supportive and safe environment possible. You also need to know what to do if your cat does hurt itself, along with what physical symptoms should prompt you to see your friendly neighborhood veterinarian as soon as possible. This chapter will discuss ways to safeguard your cat's health, including basic first-aid techniques as well as in-home care that could end up saving you a trip to the vet, or forestall serious complications of illness if you are temporarily unable to get to a vet in a timely fashion.

Annual Checkups at the Vet

Your vet will possibly be the most important person in your cat's life, next to you. Many illnesses that can hurt or kill your little feline friend can often be headed off at the pass simply by being diagnosed and treated properly. A good vet is worth his or her weight in gold, believe me. Once you find a good one, try to nurture a good, mutually respectful relationship, and learn as much as possible without being a pest.

Make sure to take your cat in for a checkup at least once each year, even if it appears to be in the peak of health at the time. During these annual checkups, your vet will give your feline a thorough physical exam, which should include:

- Examination of the cat's body, from nose to tail. The vet will search for lumps, growths, swelling, skin or hair abnormalities, parasites, or abscesses.
- Weighing the cat and taking its temperature.
- Listening to the cat's heart and lungs.
- Checking the cat for abnormal discharges from any of the bodily orifices, including the eyes and nose.
- Determining the condition of the cat's teeth, gums, and ears, as well as the scent of the cat's breath (often a sign of sickness).
- Inspecting the cat for parasites or abscesses.

In addition, the vet will palpate (or feel) the cat's internal organs to check for infection, and will also test the cat's skin elasticity to determine if it is dehydrated. He or she may take a fecal sample from the cat (often requested beforehand, at the time that you call to make the appointment), and test to determine if there is a parasitic infestation. If you schedule a visit because of a suspected illness, your vet may also take blood and urine samples for testing (the vet will probably be able to express some urine out of the cat by gently squeezing its bladder).

Any needed vaccinations or booster shots will then be administered; these will ensure that your feline is immunized against potentially life-threatening diseases. These vaccinations introduce a harmless form of disease-causing viruses or bacteria into the cat's body. These cause the cat's immune system to produce antibodies that protect the cat from the real disease. Subsequent booster shots are necessary to build a cat's immunity up to a sufficient level.

Kittens will receive their first vaccinations at about eight to ten weeks of age, then receive boosters about one month later. Boosters are then given annually for the rest of the cat's life. The rabies vaccine is slightly different; it is given first at about three months of age, boosted at one year, then repeated at three-year intervals.

Your vet can also give you great advice on just about anything to do with cats; after all, he or she sees more cats in a day than you'll probably see in ten years. Your vet can give excellent advice on topics such as:

- Diet—what is healthy, unhealthy, too much or too little.
- Behavior—what is proper, what is improper, what is causing it, and how to deal with it. If your vet cannot answer your questions about a behavioral problem, he or she probably knows someone who can.

- Environment—what is safe and unsafe, what is toxic and nontoxic, what the best litter is, etc.
- Neutering—how important it is to the health of your cat, and why you should have it done today.

Lastly, your vet will keep accurate records of your cat's health, including vaccinations, treatments, surgeries, medications, and even what flea shampoo you are using. The cat's weight and body temperature will be recorded each time you visit as well. All this is important, as it may help diagnose a pattern of illness or abnormal behavior. These records will also help you in the event you move more than an hour's drive away; your vet should be happy to forward the records to your cat's new vet, helping him or her become familiar with your pet.

A Safe, Clean Environment

Ensuring that the cat's home environment is safe, secure, and clean is one of the easiest ways to prevent illness in your cat. A home that has toxic plants, chemicals, and dangerous substances left out in the open is one that will almost certainly cause your cat to become ill at some time. Remember that cats are curious about their environment and will investigate everything, sniffing, touching, and tasting whatever they can. It is your job to protect your cat from harm.

Keeping the home clean and free of infectious germs is also an important step in preventing poor health in your cat. Dusting and vacuuming will keep infectious spores and parasites at bay. Keeping the cat's litter box scooped as free of waste as possible will reduce the chances of infection and house-soiling. Regularly cleaning the cat's food and water dishes to minimize bacterial buildup also helps keep kitty healthy, as does providing clean fresh water each day.

You can also prevent a number of health disorders in your cat by resisting the temptation to bring strays into your home. As sorry as we feel for these abandoned critters, it is important to remember they can be hosts to innumerable diseases and parasites that could infect, harm, or even kill your resident cat. If you are set on rescuing an unfortunate, however, do it right. Take it directly to your vet (after calling in advance), before ever bringing it into your home, and have it gone over top to bottom. The cat should receive a physical exam as well as blood, urine, and fecal tests to determine if it is carrying any contagious diseases or harmful parasites. You will have to leave the cat at the animal clinic until all test results come in, or until it is cured of all that ails it. Even if the stray is pronounced fit as a fiddle by your vet, its introduction into your resident cat's territory will cause great stress for all parties. Whatever you do decide, do not act impulsively, and do not encourage strays to come around your home by leaving food and water out for them (which will also attract rodents, raccoons, possums, and skunks).

Another way to prevent injury and illness in your cat is by not allowing it to come into contact with any aggressive animals. You might be on guard against a street-hardened stray cat coming in and beating up on your sweet little couch potato, but be tempted to allow a friend or relative to bring his or her dog into your home for a visit. Do yourself a favor and resist this insanity; ask your guests to leave the pooch in the car with the window cracked open, no matter how friendly they say it is. Otherwise the scene could erupt into a no-holds-barred fight, and, if the dog is a huge malamute or combative, prey-driven Bedlington terrier, believe me, your cat will lose, and just might be killed. Even dogs raised with cats may not take kindly to your cat, so why chance it? Save yourself some grief (and a big vet bill) and keep the pooches out!

Keeping Your Cat Active

Cats need exercise just as much as humans do. We just never think about planning exercise for our cats. Even the family dog gets to regularly go out and play catch with a Frisbee or retrieve a tennis ball. Not so with your cat, it seems. While it is true that the family cat will not fetch nearly as well as a dog, you can certainly get it moving around and working its muscles, heart, and lungs.

Some cat breeds will be more naturally active than others, and will not need prodding from you to become active. As a matter of fact, owners of such breeds as the Abyssinian or the Siamese probably wish that they could slow their little wildcats down. Owners of more sedate, reserved breeds such as the Persian or Himalayan might have a hard time getting their pets to get up off of their duffs, and are more prone to wind up with flabby little doormats or lazy lap warmers. In any case, obesity in a cat is not healthy, physically or mentally.

Keeping Good Records

Anyone with children knows that it is good practice to record all pertinent information regarding their health, particularly dates of vaccinations, what was given, when the next booster is due, etc. You should do this with your cat, too. In addition to vaccination records, keep a brief medical journal that records any sicknesses or traumas your cat has suffered, their duration, treatment, and date of occurrence. Write down just what medications were used, along with their effectiveness and side effects, if any. A record like this will help you and your vet determine if any patterns of illness or allergic reactions are occurring. Often this type of journal can expose to your vet pertinent clues to a chronic condition that might have remained hidden otherwise.

Also, consider writing down your cat's weight on a month-to-month basis, and pair this with the amount of food the cat eats daily. As your cat ages, you may begin to see its weight creep up as the amount of food served remains static, a sign of a slowing metabolism. This will be your cue to start cutting back on the food, or else switch over to a lower-calorie version. In addition, record the brand of food and any changes you make throughout the cat's life. This may also help spot a subtle allergic reaction in the making, or allow you to associate a specific food switch with a change in elimination habits.

Aging

Aging occurs in all animals, cats as well as humans. None of us are really all that fond of it but there is no getting around it. Our bodies age owing to degradation of our cells over time; they fail to repair themselves as efficiently over a number of years. The mechanism of aging is not understood all that well, but medical science does seem to be extending the lives not only of humans, but their pets as well. Many humans live well into their eighties now, and some past that. Cats are living longer, too; twelve or thirteen used to be considered ancient, whereas now cats living to the late teens or even age twenty are not unheard of.

A healthy, well-cared-for cat can age almost imperceptibly. It may come as a shock to you to one day realize that your feline friend is twelve or thirteen years old! Where did all the time go? Few signs of old age are glaring; most cats slow down so gradually that we hardly notice until we perhaps spot a new kitten next door at the neighbor's and see for ourselves how our "old timer" has really begun to put on the coaster brakes.

If you pay close attention, you will see the telltale signs. An older cat may begin to put on some weight as its metabolism slows (though often this gets balanced out by a waning appetite). Sometimes its eyes will cloud slightly, a result of the lenses losing moisture and becoming thicker. The cat's coat may become slightly less dense, and may have a tendency to dry out more easily. Its skin may become flakier, and may suffer more bouts of dermatitis or parasitic infestation. Few cats actually turn gray, however, unlike dogs or humans.

Possibly due to diet and its contribution to the formation of plaque and tartar, a cat can, just like a human, lose teeth during its lifetime. Some cats, particularly those fed on a canned-food-only diet, may lose several, whereas a cat raised on a predominantly dry-food diet might not lose any. Of course the owner who regularly cleans his or her cat's teeth will see far fewer feline dental problems, as will the owner who takes the cat in to the vet for a thorough cleaning once every two years.

The cat's senses very gradually become less acute over time, but again, it happens so gradually that it is hard for you or the cat to really notice until late into the cat's life. Hearing, particularly the ability to detect high frequency sounds, diminishes later on in the cat's life. The eardrums tend to thicken and lose some of their elasticity as well. Vision weakens; as stated before, the lenses thicken and cloud, decreasing the amount of light that reaches the retina. Just as in humans, the ability to discern different tastes also diminishes, as does the production of saliva. Combined, these factors can lead to the consumption of more food in order for the cat to feel satisfied. Or the cat may also lose interest in its normal food, favoring something with more intense flavor appeal (like your tuna sandwich). The older cat's sense of smell is somewhat diminished, but not by much. Its touch sensitivity remains fairly constant, perhaps right to the end; cats may even rely on touch more in old age due to the failing of the other senses.

The cat's internal workings change with age as well. As in humans, the bones of the skeleton become more porous and brittle, increasing the chance of a break or fracture. Flexibility decreases, and joints become stiffer and susceptible to arthritis. The cat tends to gradually lose muscle mass (while possibly gaining fat). The cat's reaction times slow; those old-time mousing champs just might not be able to get the jump on those little rodents anymore (but they shouldn't be outside, anyway). Brain function also suffers somewhat, with reduced memory capacity.

The cat's immune system and general resistance to infectious disease decreases, opening up the animal to various disorders, including cancer. Mucous membranes dry out and lung efficiency declines, making activity more strained, and increasing the likelihood of respiratory illnesses, including bronchitis and pneumonia. The heart is also weaker than it once was, and the circulatory system not as efficient. The cat's liver and kidneys do not function as well, leading to urinary tract problems and various chemical imbalances.

The stomach and intestines do not do as good a job of processing and absorbing food as they once did, leading to possible gastritis, diarrhea, constipation, nutritional deficiencies and (yes) gas. Feline disorders particular to the aging cat include:

- Cancerous tumors, especially among unneutered cats.
- Loss of appetite—the old cat may just not eat with the same vigor it used to when it comes to dinnertime. Try adding some odorous foods (such as sardines or fish oil) to the meal.
- Thyroid disease—hyper- or hypothyroidism is common.
- Electrolyte deficiency, or a lack of potassium due to kidney and liver failure, causing weight loss, lethargy, and anemia. Supplementation with potassium pills can often cause marked improvements.
- Diabetes, caused by reduced function of the pancreas. Oral supplements of insulin are often enough to combat this condition in the aging feline.
- Arthritis, or inflammation from wear and tear on the joints, causing pain and restriction of movement.
- Constipation, stemming from the decreasing efficiency of the cat's stomach and intestines, as well as failing activity in the colon. The addition of fiber to the diet, as well as a vet-approved laxative, can help.
- Cataracts, the substantial clouding of the lenses of the eyes, which can obscure vision in the older cat. Surgery can help.

Changes in the Routine of the Older Cat

What routines should you change in order to make the older cat more comfortable? Some suggestions include:

Temperature Regulation

The cat becomes more sensitive to fluctuations in the temperature as it ages, especially with regard to cold winter weather. Staying warm becomes crucial. Wet, damp, chilly situations should be avoided; if your cat has been used to being out in an unheated garage or basement, you might want to keep it from frequenting these areas too often. Keep it in the nice, dry, warm home instead. Likewise, if your cat has been an outdoor animal all its life, you should consider moving it indoors, even if it objects. Sub-freezing winter days and nights are no place for a twelve-year-old cat. How would you like to be outside all the time when you are eighty years old, suffering from arthritis? Consider getting your aging kitty a comfy bed if it doesn't yet have one, and doesn't sleep with you in your bed. Those cats suffering from structural problems or arthritis might even need to periodically rest on a pillow with a hot water bottle or heating pad underneath. Just make sure that the cat does not chew on the power cord.

Diet Changes

The cat's diet may need to be monitored, for several reasons, including:

- Avoiding obesity. Switching to a lower-calorie food will prevent obesity in the cat with a slowing metabolism.
- Preventing weight loss due to indifference or failing taste buds. You may need to try different foods with a cat that seems to be losing weight.
- The effects of tooth and gum problems on eating habits. Going to a softer food for those cats with missing teeth can help. Try soaking dry food in warm water for a few minutes, or go to a can-based diet.
- Dealing with the increasing difficulty the cat may have in digesting food. You may need to serve smaller, more frequent meals, to create less strain on the cat's system. A teaspoon of olive oil once each day can help move things along as well.

Grooming and the Older Cat

The aging cat may not groom itself quite as efficiently as it once did, due to stiffening joints and a reduced flexibility. You can help it by continuing to brush and comb it each day, and by keeping it as clean as possible. If your senior kitty gets dirty, do not wait for it to clean itself. Help it along with a bath or brushing. When brushing or combing, however, do so a bit more gently than when the cat was young, as the skin may be more sensitive and the coat thinner.

The Aging Cat's Litter Box

Continue to keep the aging cat's litter box as clean as possible, and consider lowering the height of the lip if it appears that the cat is having a hard time getting in and out. In a dog/cat home that has the litter box situated up high, perhaps on the top of a tall piece of furniture, you may need to relocate the box, to accommodate an old cat who cannot jump as high anymore. Place it in a room with the door propped open just enough to allow entry for the cat but not the larger dog (of course this won't work with a Chihuahua).

Keep the Old Cat Home!

Keep your elderly cat in the home, not only to protect it from the elements, but also because it can no longer move as fast as when young; an old cat might not be able to get out of the way of a speeding Buick, or could get beaten to the tree this time by Paulie the pit bull.

Thinking Twice about New Company

Avoid getting a new, frisky, active pet while your resident senior cat is still around. The younger cat, in its desire to play, will annoy the older cat, perhaps causing itself to overexert itself or get stressed out. Let it live out its golden years in peace, free from competitive tension.

CHAPTER 6

Bad Kitty: Problem Behaviors and How to Correct Them

Whenever your cat's behavior clashes with your expectations and causes you some sort of displeasure or hardship, it is, in my definition, misbehaving. "Behavior" is of course a relative term; just because your cat is not acting the way you want it to in your home does not mean it is behaving improperly for a cat. If a tiger in the wild readily walked up to a human and playfully rubbed up against him or her, that would be "misbehaving" for a tiger (and sobering for the human). Marking and scratching are completely natural behaviors in the wild, and are only improper in the home because we have deemed them so. That said, we as owners determine what is proper and improper, and then apply these standards to our cats.

Cats that behave incorrectly in the home can get in a lot of trouble with us; there is nothing more upsetting than a cat using your bed as a litter box, or biting a visitor who innocently tries to pet it. Repeat offenders often find themselves dropped off at a shelter and put up for adoption, or, in some cases, euthanized. It's not that their owners were cruel, but rather that they were at the ends of their ropes and didn't know what else to do.

Domestication of any animal, when it comes right down to it, goes against its natural programming. When you ask cats to adapt to a smaller, far less stimulating environment than their wild ancestors were used to, it reduces the number of natural behaviors that they can exhibit. This can create boredom and stress, resulting in "problem" behaviors. There are other causes for problem behavior, though, apart from this forced adaptation to a domesticated, indoor environment. Improper treatment by an owner, genetic predisposition, improper or shortened socialization, and even illness can cause major behavioral changes in a cat, resulting in friction with you, the owner. Often, a combination of causes will create a problem behavior; solutions are therefore not always easy. Other problems can be corrected fairly easily, with straightforward ways to reduce or eliminate many of the most common problem behaviors shown by domestic felines today.

Err on the side of caution. Many odd behaviors that appear suddenly are the result of some physical problem, and can be corrected through medical attention. You will correct a bad behavior and possibly save the cat's life in the process. Remember: medical first, behavioral second.

Also, never hit your cat, no matter what it has done, unless you are defending yourself or another. Hitting your cat will destroy the trust you have both developed over the years; your cat will probably be wary of you for the rest of its life. There are other more effective ways to correct its behavior. Hitting is just an expression of your frustration and anger, and always compounds existing problems.

Far and away the most common behavioral problem in cats, their urinating and defecating outside of the litter box is also one of the most obnoxious and upsetting experiences an owner can go through. The first step in diagnosing why your cat is not using its litter box is to determine if it is improperly eliminating or actually marking territory (marking can involve spraying urine or defecating, but is more likely to be spraying). To do this, you will need to catch the cat in the act at some point. If it is squatting, then the cat is urinating, not marking (true for males and females). When a cat marks, however, it remains standing and backs up to the surface to be "anointed." This spraying usually involves less volume of urine than does elimination, and will often be directed higher up on some vertical surface. It will also be much more odorous than regular urine. The sprayed urine is mixed with glandular secretions called pheromones, which impart a profoundly gamey, acrid smell.

Medical Problems

Before you assume that your cat is having accidents because it wants to make your life miserable, you need to rule out any chance your pet has some type of medical problem that has as one of its symptoms either incontinence or diarrhea. At the first sign of problems, take your cat into the vet to be examined. It could have a bladder infection, kidney problem, food allergy, sphincter weakness, or some other condition that causes the animal to soil the house. Ruling out a medical condition will bring you closer to solving the problem, and is the only fair way to proceed. (Note: Common feline illnesses are discussed later in this book.)

Nonmedical Problems

If you have ruled out a medical problem, and have decided to first treat the undesirable behavior as simply improper elimination and not marking behavior, there are numerous possible causes and solutions.

A Dirty Litter Box

Your cat's litter box should be scooped clean of waste at least once each day, and the litter replaced completely at least once each week. You should scoop and change litter more often, though, if more than one cat is using the same litter box. Owners who allow their cat's litter box to become filled with waste are just asking for trouble; remember that cats are fastidious, and will avoid a filthy box in favor of a nice clean flower pot or laundry basket. Keep the box as clean as possible, and consider getting an extra one if you have more than one cat. Also make sure to clean the box itself with mild soap and water each week, whenever you change the litter. (Note: The area where the cat has improperly eliminated must be thoroughly cleaned and treated with an "odor neutralizer"; available at all pet shops, this product will neutralize the smell of the cat's waste. If this is not done, the odor will attract the cat and cause repeated accidents.)

Changing Brands of Litter

Once your cat has gotten used to a certain brand of litter, you should stick with it. Owners who abruptly change brands of litter because of price, convenience, pretty packaging, or a nice new perfumed smell often find their cats objecting in a most objectionable manner. If your cat has suddenly decided to avoid its litter box, and you have just recently changed litter brands, go back to the old type and see what happens. If you must for some reason change brands, do so very gradually, over a three-to four-week period. Cats are finicky and very set in their ways. The more static their environment, the happier they will be.

A Change of Box

Even going to a different style of litter box can often throw a cat into a tizzy, causing it to eliminate outside of the box. If it ain't broke, don't replace it! Do not buy a new box because you think it is neat or pretty. If you insist on doing so, keep the old box around for a while; put the new one (filled with the cat's favorite litter) next to the old one, and let the cat decide. It may choose to switch, use both, or stay with old faithful. If the cat seems to like using the new box, wait a few weeks, then remove the old one.

Relocating the Litter Box

Your cat wants its litter box right where it has always been. Keep it there, if at all possible, for as long as you live in that home. How would you like it if someone kept moving your bathroom around each day? Owners who suddenly relocate their cats' litter boxes are only asking for trouble; remember, cats like the status quo! If you simply must move the box, first place an identical litter box, with litter, in the new location, and make sure the cat discovers it. Leave both boxes out for a few weeks, and watch to see if the cat is using the new one at all. If it begins to on a regular basis, you can go ahead and remove the old one. But again, try to keep things as static as possible!

Litter Box Too Close to Food Dish or Sleeping Area

Cats will not eliminate near where they eat or sleep. Do you blame them? If you have placed the litter box too close to either of these places, you may be asking for trouble. Make sure the box is located as far as possible from both of these coveted areas. When relocating it, do so gradually, and make sure you show the cat where the box is.

Litter Box Too Close to Hectic Activity

How would you like to have to relieve yourself in the middle of the an interstate highway? Makes you nervous just thinking about it? Good. That's how your cat feels if its litter box is located in a high-traffic area such as a hallway, busy kitchen, or living room. Place it instead in a quiet part of the home, perhaps a second bathroom upstairs or a little-used study. Also, avoid placing the box in an area of the home too close to lots of outside activity. If you know, for instance, that the east section of the home borders a busy street, do not place the box on that end. Opt for the quieter west section, which may border a backyard instead.

Changes in the cat's environment, apart from its litter box, can affect its elimination habits also.

MOVING

Relocating to a different home can be very traumatic for a cat; you have ripped its familiar territory right out from under it and replaced it with an alien one that certainly looks, smells and is laid out differently from what it was used to. Being suddenly brought to a strange new territory is a very serious matter to cats, who do not voluntarily change locations unless no other alternative presents itself. Making this choice for your cat is like transferring your child to a new school across town. In addition, the new home may have the old scent of previous animals; your cat may initially decide to mark over this to claim its new territory. New homes also need to be learned by your cat, just as you yourself do not feel comfortable in a new neighborhood until you have learned your way around and met the neighbors.

When moving to a new home, make sure you bring with you much of the old furnishings, carpets, and other reminders that all contain the smell of the old home; this will ease your cat somewhat. Make sure to use the same brand of litter and the same old litter box, and bring all of the cat's old toys with you, too.

If your cat begins to have house-soiling problems immediately after moving to the new place, you may need to try confining it to one room for a while until it calms down and gets used to the smell of the new place. The confinement need only occur when you are not there to supervise and when you are retiring for the night. Put the litter box in one corner of the room and see what happens. (Do not put the cat's food in there; it will be too close to the litter box. Instead, feed the cat outside of the confinement room when you come home.) If the problem continues, you may need to further reduce the cat's "living" area by using a wire mesh cage of at least 3' × 3' × 5' dimensions. Place the litter box in one corner and make sure there is comfortable flooring for the cat to walk on, perhaps some short carpeting or artificial turf. This reduction in living area should do the trick; your cat will want to avoid fouling the small area that it is living and sleeping in. Once it begins to reliably use the litter box again, expand its living space to one room for a few days, then to two, then finally back to the entire home (or whatever portion you desire).

Moving, by the way, is a great time to change an indoor-outdoor cat over to indoors only. Liking the outdoors is simply a learned behavior for a domestic cat, and what has been learned can be unlearned in time. There is no instinctive need for a cat to go outdoors unrestricted; if you wish to allow your cat out, do so by using a harness and leash, so that you can supervise it, just as you would with a dog. Remember, cats are not magical creatures who can resist infection, parasites, automobiles, and loose dogs. Try using the one-room confinement technique for a week or two, then expand your cat's space. If you insist on letting the cat out again in the neighborhood, do not do so for at least one month; get it used to its new home before you send it out into a strange neighborhood. By getting it used to the new home first, you will give it a secure place to escape to if it gets into trouble outside.

Vacations

Leaving your cat for extended periods of time can upset it, resulting in house soiling and destructive behavior. If at all possible, try not to board your cat out of the home while you are gone; this can really throw cats for a loop. They come back feeling stressed and indignant: how dare you leave them in that loud, smelly place filled with dangerous strangers? Once home, they often sulk and have accidents for a few days. Opt instead for a cat sitter, someone who can come into your home once or twice each day to feed and scoop litter. Allowing your cat to remain in its "territory" will minimize complications and prevent the stress that results from being around numerous strangers, unknown animals, and foreign sounds. If possible, have the cat sitter be someone that the cat knows and trusts. If they can take time to interact with the cat, so much the better. (Note: do not take your cat with you on vacation unless there is no other alternative; the stress of travel and unknown territories can really cause major problems.)

If it isn't possible to have someone come into your home while you are gone, consider boarding the cat at a friend's or relative's home, again preferably in the care of someone the cat knows and trusts. If you do resort to this, be sure to bring over the cat's own litter box, and consider having the host confine the cat to one room instead of letting it have free run of the house.

If, despite all your attempts to the contrary, your cat soils in a particular spot, for instance on a bed or in a closet, consider denying the cat access to this area permanently.

As discussed earlier, cats are very territorial creatures, and in the wild endeavor to plainly define the boundaries of their territories through marking, either by spraying urine, defecating, scratching, or by depositing scent from the many glands throughout their bodies. When a cat detects its own scent on the boundaries of its territory, it feels confident and secure. It's like seeing the freeway exit for your hometown after a thousand-mile trip. Another cat who approaches this marked territory can clearly sense exactly where it begins, and will cross this invisible line only at its own peril. Cats can in this way ensure themselves an adequate supply of prey, and also tend to reduce the chances of face-to-face conflict, which could result in injury or death.

Both males and females also mark in order to attract mates. Marking, therefore, supports the strong drives to claim territory, ensure an adequate food supply, and reproduce.

Taking a cat into your home and asking it to ignore these fundamental drives is asking a lot, but that is the price of domestication. The first time that a human fed a curious wolf or placed a fence around a herd of caribou, we began to compromise the natural instincts of animals. In exchange for giving up some of these instinctive behaviors, your kitty receives food, shelter, and companionship.

Dominant Cat Claiming Territory

Cats normally do not spray urine inside the very center of their territories; this is a very secure area normally not invaded by hostile strangers. An extremely dominant male or female cat may spray, though, especially if the home is large and there are many people coming and going.

Solutions

First, neuter that cat. An unneutered cat will spray in the home, period, especially when sensing the presence of strangers or other animals, even if they are outside! Get thee to a vet and get that male (or female; they do it too) cat neutered, unless, of course, you have grown fond of the smell of cat urine all over your living quarters.

If your cat has been spraying in the home for a long time and you finally get it neutered, it may still spray out of habit. If this is the case, try the following "aversion therapy" techniques.

1. Thoroughly clean the sprayed areas with an odor neutralizer, available at a pet shop.
2. Spray your cat with water from a plant sprayer if you catch it in the act.
3. Treat the sprayed areas with commercially available cat-repellent scents, or try spreading black pepper or Tabasco sauce.
4. Place double-sided sticky tape around commonly sprayed areas. Strips of aluminum foil, shallow pans of water, or sheets of crinkly newspaper also work well. These "booby traps" may work to stop the spraying, or may just send the cat off to another spot to spray.

5. If the booby traps and repellents all fail to stop the spraying, try placing small dishes of dry food near where the cat likes to spray. Cats do not like to spray near food, so this may help them break the habit. Make sure to remove the booby traps if you use this food technique.

If none of these techniques reduce or eliminate spraying by the dominant cat, you will need to reduce its territory by confining it to a room or large wire cage for a week or two, and then slowly reintroduce it to the rest of your home, one room at a time. Minimizing its territory gives the cat less reason to spray. The truly incorrigible sprayer may need to be permanently confined to a small section of the home for months before the offensive habits finally ceases. Of course you can avoid the whole ordeal by having the cat neutered before six months of age.

INDOOR-OUTDOOR CAT WHO SPRAYS RANDOMLY INDOORS

Any cat allowed to go outside the home will develop a religious habit of spraying its outside territory, whether it is neutered or not. The outside areas are the outer ranges of its territory, where most spraying goes on. By allowing your cat to go outside, you inadvertently encourage it to develop the habit of spraying. Though relatively unlikely to spray in the home, the cat will have the behavior solidly learned, and is more likely to spray inside than a cat who stays indoors.

Solutions

1. Neuter.
2. Clean all sprayed areas with an odor neutralizer.

3. Avoid letting your cat out, right from the start. Roaming is dangerous, and builds bad habits. If your cat already goes outside, break it of the habit by keeping it inside from now on. The cat will object for a few months, but it will ultimately live a healthier life and, because of the more easily secured indoor territory, will need to spray less or not at all. There will not be any competition.
4. Be prepared to use any or all of the aversion techniques described in the previous section on dominant-cat spraying.

"Invasion" of Home by Strangers

Even the most confident, secure cat can become an indoor sprayer if a new animal or person is suddenly introduced into the home. This is an invasion of the cat's core territory; it considers this a major threat, and may spray in response.

Solutions

1. Neuter.
2. Thoroughly clean with an odor neutralizer.
3. Introduce a new animal very slowly, using the crating/confinement technique mentioned in this guide. Any sudden introduction of a new cat or dog will result in spraying and fighting, so go slow.
4. Introduce your cat to a new roommate well before he or she moves in. Have the new person visit and bond with the cat first, and let him or her leave a piece of clothing behind to introduce the new scent into the cat's world.
5. Be prepared to use any or all of the aversion techniques described earlier.

The Nervous Cat

A naturally timid or nervous cat does not need much to stress it out. Often just a quick visit from a stranger will be enough to cause abnormal behavior, including spraying. A nervous, unsure cat may spray as a way to comfort itself with its own scent, as if saying "there's no place like home, there's no place like home . . ."

Solutions

1. Clean all areas with an odor neutralizer.
2. Create the most safe, secure environment possible for your cat.
3. Socialize your cat from kittenhood with as many friends, family, and easy-going animals as possible. Desensitizing the cat to the presence of strangers will help prevent this type of nervous spraying.
4. Use aversion techniques if necessary, but exclude the most sudden ones such as the mousetrap under the newspaper, or perhaps even the water spray, as these may stress the cat even more.

Moving

Relocating to a new home can instigate a cat into spraying. It is a new, strange territory that must be claimed by your cat before it can feel comfortable.

Solutions

1. Neuter.
2. Clean the carpeting in the new home with an odor neutralizer if others have lived there before you to eliminate the odor of pets who may have lived there previously.

3. Confine your cat to one room for a few days until you are sure that it is not spraying. Then watch it carefully after introducing it into the rest of the home.
4. Use any or all aversion techniques if necessary.

Remodeling

When you change the look of your home, you are changing your cat's territorial layout. It seems different to the cat, and a bit alien, especially if you replace furniture, paint the place a different color, or move things around. This change can sometimes provoke a cat to spray as a response to the new, unfamiliar surroundings.

Solutions

1. Remember that cats like the status quo. Keep things as stable as possible; if you do need to change things around, try doing so gradually, one room at a time. Do not replace all the furniture at once, and avoid buying used furniture that could have the scent of other animals on it.
2. Clean all sprayed areas with an odor neutralizer.
3. Use any or all aversion techniques necessary.
4. Confine the cat to one room, if necessary, for one week, then reintroduce it slowly.

Stray Cats Outside Your Home

The regular presence of cats outside your home may provoke your cat to spray inside as a way of confirming its territorial status in the face of possible "invasion." Dominant or insecure cats alike may spray indoors when aware of an outside cat presence. This spraying will usually occur at or near doors or windows. If your cat is unneutered it may spray to let the outside cats know that it is ready and willing to mate.

Solutions

1. Neuter.
2. Do not encourage cats to come around your home by feeding them or keeping a food dish outside for your cat's use.
3. Use a commercially available cat-repellent outside of the home.
4. Do not let your cat outside.
5. If necessary, restrict your cat's access to windows and doors by using any or all of the aversion techniques.
6. Speak to your neighbors and ask them not to let their cats come onto your property.
7. If all else fails, confine your cat to areas of the home that do not border the outside.

Cats in the wild scratch their claws on trees, posts, or whatever is available, to loosen old claws. The behavior is, however, largely a marking behavior normally occurring at the outer boundaries of a cat's territory. Raking its claws on an object leaves not only visual evidence of the cat's presence but scent evidence as well, for cats have scent glands in their paws. It is a neat, effective way of broadcasting to other cats that "these are the boundaries of my digs; keep out or we will be mixing it up." Perfectly normal in the wild, this defacing behavior does not transfer all that well to the home. Nothing is more upsetting than coming home after a long day to find your new sofa shredded to confetti. Fortunately, this is not a hard behavior to understand or change.

Your cat needs to scratch while in the home. How can you tell what the reason for the scratching is, though? Generally, if the scratching is being done in one spot, you can be pretty sure that the behavior is one of "claw conditioning" and general stretching. If, however, the scratching is being done in numerous places, particularly at or near doors and windows, then chances are your cat is marking its territory.

Providing Your Cat with an Appropriate Scratching Alternative

The first and most important step you can take to minimize destructive scratching is to first recognize that scratching needs to be practiced, and in knowing this provide your feline with a place or places to scratch to its heart's content.

Techniques to Discourage Your Cat from Scratching in the Wrong Places

You can reduce or stop improper scratching incidents in the home by trying any or all of the following:

1. Spray your cat with a stream of water from a plant sprayer when you catch it in the act. Try to do this from six to eight feet away, so that the cat does not directly associate the water with you. Timing is important; the water should hit the cat just as it begins to scratch so that it will think that scratching the object is actually what caused the unpleasant stream of water.

2. Treat the most abused objects in the home with a commercially available cat repellent, which will have an odor unpleasant to the cat. Black pepper, Tabasco sauce, or mothballs will also do the trick.

3. Place double-sided sticky tape on the most commonly scratched areas. Most cats hate the sticky feel of it on their feet, and will decide simply to move on. You can also try crumpled sheets of newspaper or aluminum foil, which will also impart an undesirable feeling underfoot. If these do not work, consider purchasing a "Scat Mat" at the pet shop. This device, which comes in varying sizes, is simply a flat plastic mat capable of delivering a very mild electric shock when the cat steps or sits on it. Placing this mat at the point where the undesirable scratching is going on will certainly dissuade the cat. (Note: the shock delivered by this device is nowhere near strong enough to hurt the cat; it simply creates a slight tingling sensation that cats find annoying.)

Try any or all of these for six to eight weeks before considering alternatives. Remember that none of these deterrents will work properly unless you also provide your cat with a proper alternative, so make sure you have good scratching posts on hand, and always encourage and reward the use of them.

Claw Shields

A product now on the market can prevent the cat's claws from doing any damage. These plastic shields glue onto the cat's nails, preventing them from ripping up your sofa, drapes, or other furnishings. They are not easy to apply, however; your vet may need to attach them for you. They also need to be replaced about every six to eight weeks, coinciding with the shedding of the old nails. Most cats hate the shields at first but eventually learn to tolerate them. Though more time-consuming, they are a valid alternative to surgery.

Getting a Finicky Cat to Eat

Dog owners rarely have problems with their pets not eating, except for the occasional spoiled-to-death toy breed, who may only be in the mood to eat when served caviar on bone china, and only when the light is just right. Some cats, however, have developed the reputation for being finicky eaters, and it is my contention that we as owners must take full responsibility for creating this problem.

Cats in the wild are not finicky; a leopard does not say, "What, monkey again?" It eats what it can kill, and is happy for it. That same leopard does not eat whenever it wants to; there is no magical, always-filled-to-the-brim "prey" dish available to it. Often it will for go days without a substantial meal. Do you think a 300-pound leopard who hasn't eaten for two days is going to be finicky? Not!

The point is, we make our cats finicky by free-feeding them, which drastically reduces their hunger drive. If you always had food available to you and ate a little of it every forty-five minutes or so, you really wouldn't ever get very hungry, and you wouldn't eat more than a handful each time.

Solutions

1. Feed your finicky cat at regular intervals to restore its natural hunger drive. Your cat will begin to look forward to mealtime and be less finicky. Plus, you will have created a way to get your cat to learn desired behaviors in exchange for a well-timed food reward. Those rewards will mean much more to a scheduled feeder than to a free-feeding cat.
2. If your cat suddenly become a very finicky eater or stops eating completely, see your vet. There might be some medical problem that needs to be identified and treated, and only a

trained doctor can do this. For example, an underactive or overactive thyroid gland can affect eating habits, as can allergies, diabetes, and intestinal blockages.
3. Put the severely underweight cat on a regular feeding schedule to increase its hunger drive, and supplement dry food with some canned food to increase its caloric intake.
4. Weigh your cat each month and keep track of any changes. Do this by picking the cat up, weighing the both of you, then weighing yourself and calculating the difference. Ask your vet what he or she thinks a proper weight for your cat should be and vary its allotted food intake accordingly to maintain this weight.
5. Limit stress on the cat as much as possible by sticking to the status quo. This will help prevent abnormal eating habits that result in an anorexic condition.
6. If you have more than one cat in the home, each will have its own idea of how much food it wants to eat. If one is a real porker and the other is skinny and finicky, the hefty one is very likely to quickly eat all its food and then start on the other cat's, while the other cat is off daydreaming or being difficult. If this is the case, consider feeding your cats in different locations to ensure that each gets the right amount and is given enough time to finish. Some are fast eaters and some are slow; take this into consideration.

Don't wait until your cat is three years old before you begin to use these techniques. Start when it is still young, before it's had a chance to develop any bad habits.

Those of you who allow your cats to have unsupervised access to the outside have undoubtedly been brought little furry or feathery "gifts" from time to time. Normally dropping these at the front door but sometimes bringing them indoors, many cats feel that they need to show off their hunting skills by showing you (whom they consider their parent or sibling) what they killed that day, be it a mouse, sparrow, or squirrel. Often the poor little creatures are still alive when delivered!

Aggression

Aggression is a part of every animal's life. It is regrettable, but predictable and unavoidable in some circumstances. For example, if a hapless, good-meaning golden retriever comes frolicking up to a female cat with a litter of four kittens, it will get into some serious trouble, believe me. That is just a mother protecting her young, one of the oldest and most justifiable forms of aggression around. Likewise, if one cat brazenly and foolishly invades the territory of another, it will in all likelihood have a fight on its hands. Completely normal stuff, as far as nature is concerned. It is only when we step in and try to apply a universal doctrine of peace and nonviolence to our pets that we run into trouble.

Much of the upsetting and unwanted aggression that we see in cats can be caused in part by our efforts to domesticate an animal that is perhaps wild at heart. Cats who are forced to deal with too many other pets in the home, as well as cats who are improperly socialized or tormented by children, can all show marked signs of aggression stemming from the stress of these situations.

Aggression in cats can also be very abnormal. Some cats are born with a genetic predisposition toward aggression, while others are so inherently timid that they can't help but act aggressively in many circumstances as they fear being hurt or killed. Still others are by nature so dominant that they can't avoid conflict with other cats that they feel they should lord over.

Whether "normal" or "abnormal," aggression in cats can be upsetting and dangerous to an owner who does not understand it or is not prepared for it. Reacting incorrectly to aggression in your cat can intensify the behavior rather than reduce it. As it is the most common problem behavior next to house soiling, understanding the different types of aggression and their causes will make you a much better cat owner. In this section, we will define the many types of aggression, their causes, and possible methods you can use to minimize or completely prevent their occurrence. (Note: aggression can be very unpredictable, genetically based, and/or medically derived; if your cat shows profoundly aggressive tendencies toward you or other people, see your vet or a feline behaviorist ASAP.)

Unpredictable Biting or Scratching

Some cats will at first accept and even seem to desire petting and stroking from their owners, only to suddenly and unpredictably lash out or bite them. They seem to suddenly reach a saturation point regarding handling, and, rather than simply leaving the premises, they exhibit "corrective" aggression, as if saying "That's enough petting right now, though I may want you to pet me again in a second or two, so I'll just stay here in your lap." Confusing and upsetting to the owner, this type of manipulative aggression is not common, but does occur especially in unneutered male cats that are allowed outdoors, in adopted strays, and in poorly socialized cats.

Cats who display this type of behavior may be suffering from a type of "schizophrenic" dilemma; they love the feel of being petted and stroked, but may be just insecure enough to fear being handled for too long. A cat that has a hard time trusting may exhibit this "yes means no" behavior. Remember that cats are solitary creatures; in the wild, few adult cats tolerate any contact at all.

You can help prevent this behavior from occurring by:
1. Neutering early.
2. Keeping your cat indoors.
3. Choosing a kitten wisely, then desensitizing it to touch, including grooming, from an early age.
4. Socializing your cat early on, with as many different people as possible.

If your cat is already showing this type of aggressive behavior, you should:
1. Limit petting and grooming sessions to just a minute or so, always stopping before the cat becomes stressed or irritated. Watch for body language cues; if you see the tail lashing back and forth, or if the ears go back and the body tenses, end the session and get away from the cat.
2. Put the cat on a regular feeding schedule instead of free-feeding it, then periodically give it treats, especially as a reward after a handling session.

With a particularly timid or unpredictable cat, simply avoid physical contact unless it requests it, by rubbing against you, for instance. Then just give it a gentle pet on the head and a treat, and call it quits.

PART 3
KITTY CULTURE

CHAPTER 7

Show Cats

SHOWING OFF YOUR PRIDE AND JOY

If you thought dogs were the only domestic pets to strut their stuff in the ring—guess again. It turns out that kitty has been wowing audiences with her meow for centuries and is now making a comeback in a big way by flaunting her fluff at both traditional shows and agility competitions.

So where are these shows? How do you enter Fluffy in a cat competition? If Fluffy isn't a purebred feline can she still compete?

A common misconception about cat shows is that they are designed only for the very best pedigreed felines. Not so. Myriad show classes range from dozens of recognized pure breeds, to the household pet class—which includes that big ball of fluff snoozing on your couch!

The very first cat show in recorded history took place in 1598 at the St. Giles Fair, in Winchester, England. The first cat shows in the United States were held at New England county fairs in the 1860s, and primarily featured the farmers' local Maine Coon breed.

Modern day cat shows are held by cat clubs, which are in turn affiliated with cat registries. The three largest registries in the United States are the Cat Fanciers' Association (CFA), the International Cat Association (ICA), and the American Cat Fanciers Association (ACFA).

Most individuals aren't aware that there are hundreds of cat shows held in the United States every year, from regional cat club shows, to major national and international events. The CFA International Cat Show is the largest international pedigreed cat show in the United States and in the Western Hemisphere. An annual event, it is held the weekend before Thanksgiving, and travels to different locations in the United States. Previous shows have been held in San Mateo, California; Houston, Texas; Kansas City, Missouri; Atlanta, Georgia; and Chicago, Illinois.

This three-day CFA event, dubbed the "Rolls Royce" of cat shows, is expected to highlight over a thousand pedigreed cats from the United States, Canada, Asia, Europe, and South America. Designed only for pedigreed cats, the show will have forty-one breeds represented, and is a must-see event for any cat lover. For more information about this show, visit their Web site at: *www.cfa.org/intl-show/*.

Kitty and Kaboodle

If you've never been to a cat show, they are generally one- or two-day events, and consist of several separate, concurrent shows and classes in show rings throughout the show hall.

Here's a rundown of the competition classes for CFA shows that include both pedigreed and nonpedigreed cats:

- Kitten Competition: for unaltered or altered pedigreed kittens between the ages of four and eight months.

- ❧ Championship Competition: for unaltered, pedigreed cats over the age of eight months.
- ❧ Premiership Competition: for altered, pedigreed cats over the age of eight months.
- ❧ Miscellaneous Competition: for breeds not yet accepted for Provisional status, but accepted for registration and showing in this class.
- ❧ Veteran Class: for any male or female, altered or unaltered, not younger than seven years.
- ❧ Household Pet Competition: for all randombred or nonpedigreed cats. Entries must have all their physical properties, and must not be declawed. Kittens must be older than four months on the opening day of the show, and those entries older than eight months must be neutered or spayed.

The household pet competition can often be the largest class in cat shows, and in general, will also tend to be the most relaxed class as there are no purebred cattery reputations at stake, and no kitten prices or potential stud fees on the line. In addition, there is no breed standard to deal with, so cats are judged on their personality, health, and general appearance. A well-groomed, happy cat of completely indeterminable lineage has every chance to do quite well in this class.

Finding Shows

If you're interested in showing your cat, start by calling a few local cat clubs for information. (If there are no cat clubs in your area, you can ask your veterinarian for help.) Internet searches will also provide you with show schedules and classes in virtually every part of the country. You can also pick up a copy of *Cat Fancy* magazine for show listings.

Before you enter your pride and joy in a show, it's highly recommended that you attend a cat show or two as a spectator. In doing so you'll have a much better understanding of the proceedings, without the added pressure of caring for your kitty in an unfamiliar situation. At cat shows you can mingle with fellow cat fanciers, ask questions, and familiarize yourself with the process of showing.

Cat shows are busy environments, so bear in mind that many breeders and judges are going to be preoccupied with their extensive duties. A little awareness and tact will go a long way in this regard, so chat with exhibitors during obvious "downtimes" and you will undoubtedly be rewarded with a wealth of information.

As tempting as it will be, you must refrain from touching the cats at shows. Exhibitors spend a lot of time and effort grooming and combing, and they probably won't appreciate stray fingers on their star attraction. You'll also notice that judges use antibacterial disinfectants on their hands after handling each cat. This helps lessen the chance of accidentally passing germs from one cat to another. If you are invited to touch an exhibitor's cat, you'll score major etiquette points by disinfecting your hands before and after petting Fluffy.

Cat Show Basics

First and foremost, before even thinking about entering your cat in a show, make sure that he's current on all vaccines. This may appear to be a little too obvious to some, but you can't take chances—the last thing you want to bring back home from a cat show is an ill feline. Some states, counties, and city jurisdictions may require proof of vaccination at the show site, so check with your show personnel early on about necessary paperwork you'll need to provide. Also, you want to be absolutely certain that your cat is free of any mites, ticks, parasites, and fleas. Good health is your cat's most precious attribute, so be confident about it before entering the ring!

In order to show your cat you'll need only a few pieces of basic equipment. A good quality cat carrier is essential, and whether you show your cat or not, it's a good idea to have one of these on hand, if only for the occasional trip to the vet or in case of emergency. Your local pet superstore will have a variety of cat carriers, usually priced very reasonably. Don't try to save a few bucks by going with the disposable cardboard models. They won't hold up for long, and should be used only as a last resort. And don't forget kitty's comfort! A fluffy towel, carpet remnant, or small pet pad makes for comfortable bedding inside the carrier.

Another requirement for showing is curtains for your cat carrier. Curtains act as sound mufflers and keep cats visually separated (a great device in helping prevent territorial disputes). You'll need to be able to curtain off the back and both sides of the carrier. If you're handy with a sewing machine, you can get as creative as you'd like with material and designs. If sewing isn't your forte, a few bath towels secured with safety pins or binder clips will get the job done just as effectively.

You'll also want to take along food and water dishes. (Nontipping styles will help keep things tidy.) Don't be too concerned if your cat doesn't eat for the duration of a show. Chances are he may be a little unnerved by the hubbub, but by providing food and water bowls, you're at least you're giving him the option. Alternately, you might bring a supply of your cat's favorite treats, which may be more appetizing than regular food on show day.

A litter pan, along with the litter that your cat is accustomed to using, is paramount. Some shows do provide litter, but cats have preferences, so stick with the stuff kitty's comfortable with.

Show rules will demand that your cat's nails are clipped. If you're uncomfortable with clipping nails, a quick trip to the vet or a professional groomer may be in order to get them clipped properly. If you decide to have a professional groomer clip your cat's nails, you may want to have them groom the kitty at the same time. Otherwise, it's up to you to bathe, comb, brush, and turn Fluffy into Miss America.

Also, to help keep your cat calm, you might toss several of his favorite toys into the cat carrier. He may not play with them at the show, but because they carry a familiar scent, he'll find them comforting.

Here's a pre-show checklist:

- Purchase a good quality cat carrier and provide curtains and bedding for the carrier.
- Make sure your cat is properly vaccinated and you have the paperwork to prove it.
- Make sure your cat is free of mites, ticks, parasites, and fleas.
- Take along food and water dishes and a supply of your cat's favorite food or kitty treats.
- Have a litter box with kitty's normal litter at the ready.
- Clip your cat's nails and have him groomed.
- Remember to bring a few of your cat's favorite toys!

Showtime!

The day has arrived and it's time for kitty to make a grand entrance. As a rule, you'll want to arrive at the show an hour before judging starts. Check in with the entry clerk, get your cage number and benching location, and then set up camp. After you and kitty are situated, locate each ring so you'll know where to be, and when.

Take note that different categories of cats will be judged at different times. The show schedule is usually printed at the back of the show catalog, so you'll know which ring you're supposed to be in next. And don't be afraid to ask for help from other exhibitors if at any time you don't understand instructions.

Once you and kitty are at your designated ring, wait until your number is called. Be aware of what ring you'll be called for next and listen for that ring's announcements. Some cat shows don't make ring announcements, so be sure you're aware of the schedule and check progress frequently.

Cats often nap during shows, so make sure your cat is awake and alert before going to the ring. A drowsy cat isn't going to show as well as an alert cat, so give him a few minutes to wake up completely. When your number is called, remove your cat from the carrier, do a little touch-up grooming, and carry kitty to the ring.

This may sound like a lot to keep track of, but don't be intimidated. Try to remember that absolutely everyone at the show had, at one time or another, their own very first show to compete in. There will be plenty of people milling about, so be friendly and open to new ideas, and have fun!

Day of show procedures:

- Arrive at least one hour before judging begins.
- Check in with the entry clerk and get your cage number and benching location before setting up.
- Check the show schedule for ring listings so you know where you need to be.
- Listen for ring announcements and constantly check the progress of the show in case of changes.
- If kitty is napping, give him plenty of time to wake up before taking him to the ring.
- Don't hesitate to ask someone if you're uncertain about a procedure or where to go!

A Brief Overview of Breed Types

In addition to providing endless entertainment, cat shows are a wonderful way to explore the incredible variety of felines in our lives. The Cat Fanciers' Association currently recognizes thirty-seven pedigreed breeds for the Championship classes, plus four breeds that currently fall into the Miscellaneous class. Each breed has a set standard for judging.

In general, breed types fall into short hair and long hair categories, with some breeds recognizing both short- and longhaired versions within the breed. Among the most common short hair breeds are the Abyssinian, British Shorthair, American Shorthair, and the Siamese. Longhaired breeds include the Burmese, Persian, Himalayan, and Siberian.

Virtually all cat breeds have common physical characteristics within each breed, and most have common personality traits as well. Exploring the nature of various breeds of felines is fascinating, and can often obliterate myths about cat origins and behavior. Here's a quick look at a few of the many interesting purebred cats you're likely to see, and their characteristics.

Naturally De-Tailed

The most recognizable, and probably the most often incorrectly identified tail-less cat, is the Manx. Cat experts and researchers generally agree that the breed originated on the Isle of Man, a tiny island between England and Ireland. No one knows for certain, but the dominant tail-less gene in this breed is probably the result of a spontaneous mutation that spread to the resident cat population on the island.

The American Bobtail is fast becoming a favorite among many breeders due to its outgoing and intelligent nature. While the tailless nature of the Manx breed is often described as an isolated mutation, the American Bobtail is generally accepted as an American breed that evolved naturally, without the influence of mutations or hybridization. This breed has been described as being extremely adaptable, calm, intelligent, and almost doglike in nature.

Wet Ones

The Maine Coon breed is one of the oldest pedigreed breeds in America, and second only to the Persian in popularity. Cat owners who are accustomed to using a spray water bottle as a corrective training device may be in for a bit of a surprise with the Maine Coon, as the stereotypical feline hatred of water doesn't apply to this big, sturdy breed. With origins in the cold northeastern United States, the Maine Coon has tufted ears and paws, and a long, shaggy, water-resistant coat. In addition to being one of the largest feline breeds, Maine Coons are also one of the gentlest in nature.

Well, Curl My Ears!

Discovered as a stray in California, the first known American Curl brought an affectionate nature and an intriguing genetic mutation to cat fanciers worldwide. The ears of the American Curl curve back in an arc away from the face, toward the center of the back of the head. This tendency was determined to be a spontaneous genetic mutation, with a dominant gene causing the ears to curl. Intelligent, affectionate, and strikingly beautiful, the American Curl is a unique and charming breed.

Little Panthers

In the 1950s, Nikki Horner, a cat breeder in Kentucky, set out to create a miniature black panther. By 1976, her efforts were rewarded by the CFA as the Bombay breed became an officially recognized championship breed. Closely related to the Burmese, the Bombay has a glossy black coat and copper eyes. Congenial and outgoing, it's a breed known for its easygoing and affectionate temperament.

Living Relics

The modern Egyptian Mau is recognizable in much of the artwork of ancient Egypt, and is commonly thought to have been bred from a subspecies of an African wild cat. Cherished as pets, worshipped as deities, and often mummified and mourned, these cats played an integral part in the lives of ancient Egyptians. Today, the Egyptian Mau has the distinction of being the only naturally spotted domestic cat breed, and as such, is one of the most striking of all breeds.

Long Hair, Short Hair, No Hair?

Sometimes viewed as a completely hairless breed, the Sphynx cat often has a thin, peachfuzzy coat akin to suede. First discovered in 1966, the hairless gene was found to be a natural genetic mutation. Careful, selective breeding has resulted in a robust gene pool, producing healthy, highly intelligent, and intensely inquisitive cats. Sometimes thought to be the feline answer to allergy-prone cat owners, the relative lack of hair on the Sphynx can actually intensify allergic reactions. Unusual and exotic in appearance, the Sphynx breed has developed an intensely loyal and enthusiastic following.

The Tip of the Iceberg

These breeds are a tiny part of the endlessly fascinating cat breeds available today. If this has whetted your interest, and you're a cat lover who is interested in buying a purebred cat then it's time to do a bit of research to find a reputable breeder. If you'd like to learn more about showing your cat or just want to research different breeds you can visit the following Websites:

> The Cat Fanciers' Association (CFA): *www.cfainc.org*
> The International Cat Association (ICA): *www.tica.org*
> The American Cat Fanciers Association (ACFA): *www.acfacat.com*

Finding Responsible Breeders

While your local pet shop may seem like the logical place to search for a purebred cat, it's not a practical avenue. Many pet shops deal with animals from "kitty mills" that breed as many litters as possible; often with little regard to solid professional breeding programs, pedigree, or history. If you're serious about a purebred feline, then start hitting the cat show circuit. Not only is it a terrific way to scout for a feline, but it's a great way to find a reputable breeder.

Most of the breeders who attend and compete in cat shows deal directly with their clientele, and don't sell their cats through third-party shops and dealers. Be prepared to answer as many questions from a reputable breeder as you're likely to ask. Good breeders want excellent homes for their kittens, and many of them will even ask you to sign a contract requiring you to care for your new feline.

Breed Rescue—A Valuable Alternative

Purebred cats can be expensive, but it is possible to get the known qualities of a purebred cat through a variety of breed rescue programs across the country. Breed rescues are typically operated by volunteers who love their particular breed, and make great sacrifices to protect and foster their charges.

Felines found in breed rescue are seldom problematic misfits. In fact, most of these cats find their way into breed rescue situations as a result of their owner becoming ill, or relocating, or from people who find themselves unable to properly care for the cat for any number of reasons.

Cats in breed rescue programs are usually taken in by volunteer foster homes, where they are evaluated for adaptability. Most breed rescue volunteers take great care in also evaluating potential new owners, so be prepared to answer a lot of questions, none of which are designed to offend you. Your breed rescue volunteer is as determined as you are to find a good home for their cats, and they want to make sure that the animal never has to go through the process again.

Local cat clubs, cat shows, your veterinarian, and often your local animal shelter are all good sources for helping you find breed rescue programs in your area, so don't hesitate to contact any of them.

International Cat Agility Tournaments

A relative newcomer to the cat show circuit is the International Cat Agility Tournaments (ICAT). ICAT is the only sanctioned organization that holds contests sanctioned by local cat show clubs. These contests have no pedigree or breed requirements, and are open to all happy, healthy cats. If you're not familiar with cat agility contests, the object is for the handler to lure or direct the cat through an obstacle course as quickly as possible.

ICAT currently has three levels of competition:

- ❧ Level 1: Basic, is a low-impact course over mostly flat terrain. It's designed for older, heavier cats, and for first timers.
- ❧ Level 2: Intermediate, is the next step for cats and owners who have some experience with the agility course.
- ❧ Level 3: Advanced, is the highest obstacle course level, designed to display the maximum level of physical ability and interaction between the cat and its handler.

Agility courses are designed to ICAT specifications, and can be built with readily available materials. Of course, you can start training your cat for agility with the obstacles in your home that he's already perfectly familiar with: jumping over couches and chairs; going under tables; and bolting through doorways. In many ways, your home is already your cat's playground, so there's no reason not to take full advantage of it!

One of the intriguing concepts in regard to cat agility is that it offers a new opportunity to expand your relationship with your cat. The developers of ICAT have proved time and again that cats respond very positively to training, and that cat agility tests are a lot of fun for you, and most importantly, for your cat.

For more details, including course specifications, visit the ICAT Web site at: *www.catagility.com*.

CHAPTER 8

Cat Psych 101

I Am Kitty . . . Hear Me Roar!

It was once said that, "Thousands of years ago, cats were worshipped as gods. Cats have never forgotten this."

No truer words were ever spoken when it comes to the feline species, and that legacy continues to expand exponentially as more individuals bring felines into the family fold. No matter the breed or the reputation, cats are amazing creatures. Few species can claim a position so well situated in history, and as such it is no wonder they have evolved into loyal and loving companions who are infinitely brilliant, and relentlessly sneaky.

In myriad cultures, cats have been both deified and persecuted. They've been presented as gods and feared as harbingers of doom, yet through it all they've persevered and become one of the most beloved species on the planet.

Five thousand years ago, Egyptians worshipped cats as demigods, and as their domestication spread among the known worlds, they quickly became just as valued for their mousing abilities as their eccentric habits. These elegant creatures have accomplished everything from guarding our precious grain, to tearing up our loveseats, to contentedly purring in our laps. They have generations of breeding and intelligence behind them, and continue to provide infinite companionship, loyalty, and mystery.

As with humans, cats range in personality and temperament, but as a whole they're a species bred to last, and more than likely outlast most owners when it comes to patience. As most cat owners can attest, it's difficult to pull the wool over a cat's eyes. They see everything, they hear everything, and they instinctively know how to outsmart the keenest intellect or overcome any evasive maneuver.

So how does one understand, much less train such a creative breast? When the king of the domestic jungle roars, does it mean he loves you or intends to shred your couch? How can one deal with a creature who feels his intellect is a hundred times greater than yours?

The bottom line is that is doesn't really matter. Cats don't discriminate when it comes to age or race—they love all equally and are quite perceptive when it comes to sensing ever-changing human moods and domestic situations. In many ways, they're the perfect companion. Aside from dogs, no other species has developed such an intimate relationship with humans . . . and it shows. Understanding the feline mind does require a bit of patience, but the benefits are well worth the effort.

It's hard to resist a cat—their alluring charm and soothing purr is comfort food for the soul. What sets cats apart from their waggy counterparts is that they're nocturnal animals who prefer a more solitary existence. In many ways, that's what makes a feline/human relationship so intense, and at times difficult to interpret. However, understanding the mind of a cat, complex though it may seem, is easy once you're able to interpret their body language and vocalizations, and begin the intimate repartee that will last a lifetime.

Meow Mixup?

It's a sunny afternoon and you're sitting in your favorite chair with a book. Across from you, Fluffy is spread out luxuriously on the couch, eyes shut, purring louder than a boat motor. You return to your book, but within minutes, Fluffy jumps on the arm of your chair, issues a glare that would melt iron, and lets out a meow that can be heard across Siberia.

You gasp.

What could it be? Is Fluffy hungry? Does her neck need nuzzling? Does the litter box need cleaning? Is the couch not soft enough? Am I wearing the wrong socks?

As your brain bogs down in a blaze of frenzied questioning, Fluffy's ears prick up, her gaze widens, and she raises her head.

Uh oh.

For every action there is an equal or opposite reaction, but how do you apply that to a creature whose body language could mean anything from "There's something floating in my water dish," to "I own you"?

Cats are misunderstood creatures; their various behaviors often being interpreted as aloof, reclusive, and even snooty. What most people don't realize is that cats communicate almost entirely through body language, vocalization, and scent. Their movements and the sounds they emit, both subtle and dramatic, are their way of telling you what's on their mind—and there's always something on a cat's mind.

Many studies have been done over the years in an effort to decode the virtue of every move and sound a feline makes. It's easy to interpret the wagging tail and bark of a dog, but cats are suave and complex creatures who linger in the sublime. Their tails, ears, legs, torsos, the way they rub against you, and a wide range of meows all come into play when a cat communicates with its owner.

Learning to interpret your cat's body language and vocalization will help you better understand your cat's needs and wants, and ultimately, it will make both of your lives easier. As a rule, use common sense when studying your cat's behavioral patterns. A cat that is purring happily with half-closed eyes is probably very happy with the way you're petting him. On the flipside, a cat whose tail is swishing and who takes a swack at you is more than likely extremely annoyed and demanding to be left alone.

Bear in mind that at all times your cat is attempting to communicate with you the best way it knows how. So pay close attention to both the verbal and nonverbal cues, and in no time you'll both be purring contentedly.

Tiger by the Tail

A cat's tail is usually a good indicator of its general mood and emotional status. A tail held high, for example, can indicate welcome, while a tail that sways gently about can represent pleasure. A tail that twitches slightly can indicate excitement, while a broad swishing motion can indicate annoyance. There are subtle but distinct differences that ultimately tell the tale about how your cat is feeling and how you should respond.

For starters, watch your cat as it walks around the house or yard. The more you watch, the better you can recognize whether your cat is excited or annoyed with you, another cat, or some other object. In time, the way your cat holds its tail will become second nature to your interpretation.

Curiosity and friendly camaraderie is likely to be the mainstay of your daily existence, but keep in mind that there are always exceptions. As most cat owners can attest, a cat whose tail is thrashing wildly is growing more and more agitated by the second. If conflict or confrontation is about to occur, cats often hold their tails straight up, the hair bristling and puffing out in an effort to appear more threatening. They may also turn sideways in order to appear larger in stature. At this point, dominant cats maintain that tail posture, while submissive cats tend to lower their tail between their legs, which can indicate fear. Learn to recognize the difference in these positions and both you and your cat will react accordingly.

Tales of the tail:

- A tail that is rigid and held high shows welcome and friendship.
- A tail that twitches generally indicates excitement.
- A tail tucked between a cat's legs or held low down indicates fear, submission or defeat.
- A tail that is raised and gently sways like a question mark indicates excitement or interest in something.
- A tail that swishes broadly from side to side shows annoyance or irritation.
- It's sometimes said that if a cat's tail quivers it's the greatest show of love they can issue.
- A thrashing tail means anger, especially if it's bristled or puffed out. Watch out!

Here Kitty Kitty...

Mr. Spock's Vulcan ears were a perfect match for his staid emotional existence. Not so for Fluffy. As much as you monitor your cat's tail movements, equal attention should be paid to its ears. A feline's ears have a wide range of motion, each position indicating a certain mood, emotion, or potential behavior. Ears can point, prick, or lay in certain ways, so take mental notes of what you and your cat are doing when you recognize these postures, because those cute furry little ears are primed for interpretation.

As a benchmark, if your cat's ears are pricked, it means he's probably interested in something, but there are other indicators that accompany this. If the ears are pricked and the head is held high, your cat is showing dominance. By contrast, pricked ears and a lowered head show submissiveness or inferiority. If your cat's head is tucked-in, you'd better start a song-and-dance, because it means Fluffy is bored!

What kitty's ears are telling you:

- Ears pointed forward show alertness or aggression.
- Ears pointed forward and in an outward position means your cat is listening to something.
- Ears that lay very flat express fear or extreme anger.
- Ears laid back can be one of two things. If the cat's body is steady it's indicative of a defensive posture—your cat is deciding what to do. If the ears are back and the body is low to the ground your cat is showing guilt or remorse.

Can You Hear Me Now?

Mary Bly said it best: "Dogs come when they're called. Cats take a message and get back to you."

As complex as cats are in terms of body language, they're equally complex when it comes to vocalization. Cats speak on their own terms and come armed with a repertoire of meows, growls, hisses, yelps, and an assortment of insanely cute purrs. In general, purring indicates pleasure, contentment, and stress relief. Meows run the gamut from greetings to curiosity, while growling, hissing, and spitting typically indicate aggressive or defensive behavior.

As owner and cat become better acquainted with one another a verbal communication will inevitably ensue. Some felines make their presence known with a range of meows Pavarotti would envy, while others choose to cut loose when making a point, when they're particularly pleased, or when issuing a specific demand like, "Feed me NOW."

On occasion you may be surprised to hear a low throaty growl or high-pitched yelp from your cat. When that occurs, it's likely that a foreign cat has entered their territory or a fight is about to erupt. Feral and stray cats often resort to these meows or frenzied hisses in an effort to intimidate or exert dominance over any cats within earshot. In addition, you may hear these types of meows if your cat is in heat.

In time, most cat owners will learn what certain vocalizations mean and be able to translate the subtle differences in tone. Playful meows or meows offering greetings will sound different from complaints or demands a cat makes, especially if food or displeasure are an issue.

Purring is yet another part of a cat's makeup that is open to interpretation. More often than not, cats purr when they're happy or relaxed, so for the most part you can assume it's a sign of contentment. However, purring can also serve double duty as cats also purr to relieve stress. A cat who is extremely ill or plagued by anxiety might purr in an effort to provide self comfort. If you suspect that is the case with your cat, consult your vet immediately, especially if breathing appears labored or the purring is accompanied by behavior uncommon for your cat.

One word of caution: If Fluffy is hissing at you like a tea kettle . . . move on and give her some space.

Smooth Moves

In general, you can tell a great deal about the way a cat is feeling from its posture, vocalization, and ear and tail position, but it doesn't stop there. Cats have an astounding repertoire of body movements, from rubbing and kneading, to stretching and sulking. All of these movements and actions are a study in feline communication, and while in some cases they may vary slightly from one breed to another, they generally represent similar moods and emotions.

I'll Be Watching You

As with most feline behaviors, eyes are also an indicator of what's brewing in Fluffy's mind. When a cat's eyes are wide open, it's safe to assume that kitty is happy, curious, or inquisitive. If their eyes are half shut, as with humans, then Fluffy is probably starting to drift off to sleep. If the pupils are dilated, then it's a good bet your cat is either scared of something, or preparing to show aggression.

The one to watch out for is if your cat shows a slight glint or gleam in their eye. At that point, start paying attention, because more than likely Fluffy is plotting something mischievous!

Like humans, cats also sulk, and at one time or another, cat owners will notice this expression. When cats are preparing for or faced with aggression, they stare at each other. A cat who abandons this stare down usually wants to avoid an altercation. But this action isn't just limited to cats—humans also have stare downs with their felines, especially if Fluffy has done something naughty. Being that humans are so physically imposing, chances are that Fluffy will break the gaze and move off to sulk. Fortunately, once she relaxes she'll get back to her normal purring and inquisitive gazing.

As a rule, your cat's eyes should be clear and bright. If you notice a change in their gaze or their eyes are half-closed despite being fully awake, contact your vet immediately, as this may indicate signs of illness.

Rub Me Tender, Rub Me Sweet

How many times have you entered a room and suddenly felt something furry brushing your shins? Did you immediately think "Wow, what a friendly cat?" Did you automatically bend down and pet kitty's head or stroke her back? A response to such a display of warmth is instinctual for both man and beast, but what you probably didn't know is that Fluffy just marked you with her scent.

The feline act of rubbing against a human's legs plays an intricate part in the cat communication dance. Felines are fine-tuned machines when it comes to scent, and they leave their mark by emitting pheromones from strategically placed glands all over their body. The glands on Fluffy's face leave a scent marker on you that serves as both a comfort zone and a reference point for other cats you come in contact with. It also serves to establish the beginnings of a relationship between you, Fluffy, your friends, family, and all other cats in your household. And let's face it—Fluffy is also claiming you as her territory!

Leg rubbing is also a reinforced behavior. If you do bend down and pet your cat every time it rubs against you, then it's likely to be a continued action. Cats are cool customers who have no qualms about repeating maneuvers that result in their pleasure. They are, after all, gluttons for grandiose moments of undivided owner attention.

Once a rubbing behavior starts, then it typically never ceases, especially if your cat realizes you're paying attention (even if you're not paying attention, you soon will be). At times, rubbing up against you may become more insistent if, for example, your cat learns that persistent rubbing or even head butting will get you to the feeding bowl faster. Felines are a quick study, and they have no problem telling you what they want and when they want it. It's your responsibility to listen and acquiesce to their needs.

Bear in mind that there are other ways that rubbing comes into play. While you may not always be sure what a cat wants when rubbing against you in a specific manner, there is one action you can be certain of: If your cat rubs your face with its own and gently moves its nose along your cheek and forehead, you are a well-loved owner! When cats greet other cats they perform this action, so for a human, it's a great honor to be acknowledged in such a manner.

Likewise, if Fluffy rolls over, exposing her belly, you're also being paid a great compliment. Some cats love to have their bellies rubbed, others may not (you'll figure that one out quickly), but either way they're revealing the most vulnerable part of their body, and that is a show of complete trust.

Rubbing or petting your cat is an extremely tactile experience for both of you. Just as humans carry their childhood memories with them into adulthood, it is said that cats retain memories of their kittyhood. A cat's urge to knead its owner is one example of this. Likewise, your cat may equate your stroking her with her mother licking and grooming her fur when she was a kitten.

All creatures great and small benefit from intimacy and attention and your cat is no exception. As you pay attention to what your cat adores, so is your cat taking notes about what comfort they can provide you.

Getting a Leg Up on Cat Communication

Another component to understanding the feline mindset is observing their leg movement. A cat's legs aren't just for walking, they also serve as an early warning system. If your cat's forelegs are bent, it indicates a defensive position—your cat would prefer not to engage in battle, but it will defend itself if necessary. If, on the other hand, your cat's legs are fully stretched, they are feeling confident and prepared to attack.

When cats feel threatened they often "puff" themselves up and turn sideways in an attempt to look bigger and hopefully intimidate potential enemies. A cat who appears fluffy and bristled is feeling confident and exuding aggression. However, that particular stance is not to be confused when it comes to kittens or senior cats. In many instances, an arched back and bristled fur of a kitten is simply an invitation to play, while for an older cat it typically means they wish to be left alone.

On the flipside, when a cat bends its hind legs it usually means indecision or timid behavior. A cat who intentionally reduces its body size by tucking its legs under itself is on the fence—it's showing submissive behavior but is ready for action should the need arise.

Knead Me?

Kneading, or treading is a common feline occurrence, especially in cats who may have been separated from their mothers too early. This particular action simulates what kittens do when attempting to incite the flow of their mother's milk. Usually accompanied by purring, a cat will push its pads into you, alternating them in turn. It's cute and it will no doubt make you feel motherly, but be warned, when Fluffy is pushing her pads into your stomach or leg, she's usually got outstretched claws!

THAT'S MINE. THAT'S MINE. THAT'S MINE!

Ever battle for couch space with a twenty-pound feline? Find yourself fighting Fluffy all night for pillow supremacy? Can't do the laundry because there's a Tom firmly planted atop your dirty duds? There's a reason for that, and just in case you weren't aware of it by now, you don't own the cat—the cat owns you.

In order for you and your cat to coexist in peaceful harmony, it is essential that you understand that cats are highly instinctual creatures. Because they communicate primarily through body language, their behaviors are often reflective of their sensitivities, their mood, and, perhaps most importantly, their established territory.

If you're a feline, real estate is the name of the game, and it doesn't matter if a cat spends its time indoors, outdoors, or shuffling between the two. In Catland, the need for staking a claim is paramount, and there are several methods cats employ when establishing prime property and prize possessions (and in case you're wondering . . . that includes you!).

The pheromones emitted from different glands on a cat's body are transmitted by rubbing motions, and while that does help establish a comfort zone, it also serves to mark territory. Felines possess a highly honed sense of smell, and being that each cat emits its own distinct scent, it makes for a distinct form of inner-species communication. (Cats use these scents both at home and in the wild as a form of identification and greeting one another.)

Just like humans have a favorite chair or pillow, cats have certain comfort zones, which can range from a certain area on a bed to a windowsill to the top of a radiator (among other odd hiding places where we can never find them). As previously mentioned, the act of rubbing against a human's legs serves double duty. When gliding gently along your shin, chances are that Fluffy is offering up a greeting or demand, but in doing so, she's also left a scent marker. The same goes for all other objects in your house or yard. When you see your cat coolly strolling about rubbing along chair legs or cushions or carpet, the cat is leaving its scent.

If you're a first-time cat owner and have only one cat, you'll be surprised to discover that Fluffy may even battle with you for territorial supremacy!

Fluffy Versus Morris

"In a cat's eye, all things belong to cats," goes the English proverb, and that is never more evident than in a multicat household where territorial dominance rules and a definite pecking order usually emerges. In general, weaker cats often fall victim to acts of aggression if they happen to cross into "enemy" territory. For example, if the perceived weaker cat heads for the water bowl when the more dominant cat is still skulking about, the dominant cat may take a swack at the intruder. The same can happen if a dominant cat claims a particular windowsill or a certain sleep zone or any number of spaces. It can also occur if both cats are vying for your attention.

Cats are part of the family and, as such, they feel they have the right to their own space. Makes sense, right? So what do you do when you plunk Morris down smack in the middle of Fluffy's surf and turf? At that point, you'd better run, because if Fluffy doesn't immediately turn tail and start tearing up the loveseat, she soon will be.

As many cat owners can attest, some cats in a multicat household (especially males) will mark their territory by urinating in an area, letting the other cats know in no uncertain terms that a territory belongs to them. Behavioral patterns in these instances take multitudes of patience and trial and error to resolve. Explaining urination patterns to your vet is a smart move, because in some instances it may mean one or more of your cats is having urinary tract problems.

If it's not a health issue, however, it's time to research the various methods and products you can use to halt the urination situation. The Internet offers a breadth of information and products when it comes to "bad kitty" behaviors and more than likely, you'll find plenty of other owners in cat chat rooms who've come up with innovative solutions.

The best approach to bringing a new feline into the fold and avoiding bad territorial behaviors is using common sense. As a rule, if you're introducing a new cat into an established household, it's best to keep the cat separated from the others for a period of time. This way kitty can take its time and familiarize itself with the sights, sounds, and scents of its adopted home before meeting the rest of your clan.

Also, keep in mind that patterns of territorial dominance and submissiveness can change. A cat who rules the roost for many years, then suddenly becomes ill can trigger a change in the hierarchy. The more you study the behavior of your cat or the interaction between multiple cats, the more you'll be able to recognize their pecking order and claimed territory. At the very least, it will definitely help you bond as a family by sharing those territories.

Changes in Behavior

Cats are highly adaptable creatures, but that doesn't mean they are immune to lifestyle changes or emotional changes that occur in a family household. Cats, like humans, develop certain routines, especially if a household contains more than one feline. If your cat is displaying odd behavior, pay close attention because the cause could be physical or environmental.

Reasons for a change in your cat's behavior vary. You may notice that your cat refuses to eat, or isolates itself from you or other cats in the household. Your cat may start looking a bit ragged or seem irritable. All of these things are signs that your cat is unhappy for a reason you have to uncover. For starters, take Fluffy to the vet to determine whether her behavior is masking illness. If she's got a clean bill of health, then it's time to dig deeper.

First try to discern what might be upsetting your cat. Have you recently moved? Have you added family members or new pets to your household? Have you experienced more physical or emotional stress than usual? Cats are very much in tune to our lives and the emotional rollercoasters we ride. If your life becomes disrupted, chances are that your cat is feeling your residual stress.

Take stock of your physical surroundings. Indoor cats have different needs than outdoor cats. Your domicile is their world and they require plenty of hideouts and furniture to explore and lounge upon. They also love staring out windows and open spaces where they can bat toys around. Your cat's displeasure could be as simple as a lack of space or change of environment.

If you have an outdoor cat that is suddenly spending more time indoors, then you need to find out why. Does it have easy access in and out of your house? Is it threatened by a neighborhood dog or child? Is it being traumatized by recent construction?

If your cat is having a problem you need to spend time gently talking and stroking it in an effort to show how much you care. Cats have enormous hearts and they feel secure knowing they have a warm and happy home. Showing your cat patience and affection will reinforce their status in your life, and hopefully, you'll both be able to get to the root of the problem.

The Hunter and the Hunted

If your cat is an outdoor cat, then you've probably had a "gift" brought into your house at one time or another. If you're lucky, it didn't scare you to death. Hunting for prey is instinctual for a feline—they can't help it. But let's face it, finding a dead bird or mouse in your living room is nothing less than upsetting, especially if it takes off running. Fortunately, there are solutions you can employ to help your neighborhood critters survive.

Outdoor cats have more options than indoor cats when it comes to entertainment. For them, nature is one big smorgasbord of sideshows and sporting events. If Fluffy is playing Rambo and bringing back hostages by the dozen, punishing her won't help. She is, in fact, proud of her accomplishment and feels deserving of your praise (which is tough to issue when a rodent corpse is in your boot).

One solution is keeping your cat in at night, or tying a bell to its collar as an early warning system. Another way to keep Fluffy off the hunt is to provide her with a host of toys or by playing with her yourself. Cats are easily entertained, so to avoid the mouse in your house, grab a few catnip toys and let Fluffy chase them around the room.

Mutual Adoration

Some would argue that attempting to understand the mind of a cat is akin to being the patron saint of lost causes. Those folks have obviously never owned a cat. If you're not familiar with how a feline communicates, you soon will be the minute Fluffy enters your home. All it takes is a bit of observation, patience, and understanding on your part. Always remember that Fluffy is watching you as much as you are watching her. Tails may swish and various meows and stares are inevitable, but in the end, the sweetest sound you'll hear is a lovely purr that tells you Fluffy is happy and healthy.

PART 4

CAT HEALTH

CHAPTER 9

Cat First Aid

You can perform emergency first aid on your cat only if you are properly motivated and prepared. Doing so may help prevent permanent physical damage to your cat and could actually save its life. Veterinary clinics are not always open or available, so it helps to be able to take care of your cat until you can quickly get it to a vet.

FIRST-AID KIT

You should have a well-stocked first-aid kit handy to deal with emergencies as well as situations that do not necessarily require the help of a vet but need attention. If you already have a first-aid kit put together for your family, it should do just fine, though you may want to add some extra gauze roll and adhesive tape. Being able to perform simple techniques such as pulling a thorn from your cat's foot and disinfecting the wound will allow your vet to deal with more serious cases, and will save you the needless stress and expense of a trip to the vet. Keep the first-aid supplies in a small fishing-tackle box and store it in a convenient place, perhaps in a bathroom cupboard.

Taking Kitty's Temperature

One of the best reasons I can think of for handling your cat from an early age is so that, one day, you will be able to take its temperature without getting ripped to shreds. Most cats will not take kindly to this, but it is often an important part of diagnosing what is wrong with your kitty.

Clean a rectal thermometer with soap and water, rinse it well, and then shake it down to below 98 degrees Fahrenheit. Then apply a liberal amount of petroleum jelly to the tip and the first inch or so. Also place small amount of petroleum jelly on the cat's anus. While a trusty friend stands the cat on a table, lift its tail and insert the thermometer with a straight push, being careful not to put any sideways pressure on the shaft, which could break the tip. You may need to roll the thermometer between your fingertips a bit to get it inserted properly. Insert it about one inch or so, and leave it in for at least one minute. Do not let the cat run off; the thermometer could break, and you'd have one sorry kitty. Then, remove and read the results. If it reads anywhere between 101 and 102.5 degrees Fahrenheit, your cat's temperature is normal.

Taking the Cat's Pulse

The easiest place to feel a cat's pulse is on the inner surface of one of the rear legs, right where it meets the body. A large femoral artery passes close to the surface here; if you hunt for it you should find it quickly. Count the pulses for fifteen seconds, then multiply by four to get the correct beats per minute.

Cuts and Scrapes

Many injuries to the cat's skin can be effectively treated at home. The exceptions include deep wounds and those that have severed an artery and will not stop bleeding. Serious burns, breaks in the skin caused by a compound fracture, and animal bites also need the quick attention of a vet, though you can perform preliminary treatment on these injuries in the interim.

A scrape that barely breaks the skin (these will most likely appear on the cat's foot pads) can be cleaned with an anti-infective solution, then treated with an antibiotic ointment (ask your vet or pharmacist for recommendations as to what products to use). Often a bandage is unnecessary, though you will want to clean the scrape twice each day until it begins to heal and the threat of infection has passed. Be sure to reapply the antibiotic ointment each time you clean the wound. If any signs of infection appear, see your vet.

Carefully observe any wounds on your cat's chest, to ensure that there are no air bubbles in them—an indication of a punctured lung. This serious condition will require the immediate services of a vet, who may need to perform surgery to correct the problem.

Most cuts in the skin will stop bleeding fairly quickly, and can be treated by you at home. Those cuts that seem to be deep or continue to bleed for more than five straight minutes will probably need veterinary attention; your vet will want to clean and suture the wound. In the interim, though, you can help minimize the bleeding by applying direct pressure to the wound, either by pressing down directly on it with a gauze pad, or applying a pressure bandage, which is simply a gauze pad held in place with gauze roll or an elastic bandage. If the wound is on a limb or tail, for example, you can wrap the area several times (not too tightly) and leave it for fifteen minutes, observing whether or not it continues to bleed, or eventually stops. Often this short period of direct pressure will quell the flow of blood and allow clotting to begin. You will be able to carefully remove the pressure bandage and clean the wound with an anti-infective solution, being careful not to incite more bleeding. If necessary, you may need to leave a pressure bandage on for a longer period of time. If this is the case, clean the wound as best you can, then wrap it securely. If the wound is on the tail or a limb, wrap from the wound down to the end of the appendage; this will prevent swelling and minimize oxygen debt to the parts below the wound. If the wound is on a part of the cat's body that you cannot wrap, apply direct pressure to it with a gauze pad for ten minutes and see if the bleeding stops.

Some cuts or wounds will need to remain covered for a few days. If these are located on the leg or tail, wrap the entire appendage with roll gauze, then wrap over this lightly with adhesive tape (the wrap should not be as snug as with the pressure bandage, which is merely meant to stop bleeding). Change this type of bandage at least once per day, or when the cat chews it off, which will happen, believe me. If the wound is on the back or stomach, you can wrap a large white cloth around the cat's middle, tie it either on top or bottom, then secure it with adhesive tape. A wound on the neck can be protected with a handkerchief tied bandanna-style. If the cat has a wound on its face or head, you may need to fit an "Elizabethan collar" on it. It looks like a lampshade, and makes the cat look and feel silly, but it will prevent it from scratching and licking the wound.

Bandaging for Fractures or Breaks

Sprains or muscle pulls will not normally call for bandaging or splinting, but may require that the cat be confined to a crate or small room for a few days to limit movement. Even if hairline or simple fractures are present, they may not need splinting right away, but will necessitate a trip to the vet. In the case of a serious break or fracture of a leg, in which the lower portion of the leg is dangling freely, you will need to stabilize it immediately with a splint. Find a heavy piece of cardboard or another appropriately sized, stiff object to serve this purpose. Wrap the injured leg carefully (with a friend holding the cat) with cotton padding; a disposable diaper will work well. Secure this lightly with adhesive tape, then tape the splint to the padding. Make sure to cover any exposed fractures with gauze and tape to limit infection. Then get the cat to the vet, ASAP!

Tourniquets

Serious bleeding of the limbs or tail that does not respond to a pressure bandage may necessitate the use of a tourniquet, a last-ditch technique you should use while preparing to go to the vet clinic. Never a first choice, tourniquets can, if applied improperly, cut off all blood flow to all areas below the wound, effectively starving those tissues of vital oxygen. Tissue death can result; in severe cases, the affected limb or tail may need to be amputated.

Use a length of rope, surgical tubing, cloth, or even an extension cord, if that is all that's available. Form a loop or slip knot, and tighten it around an area a few inches above the wound. Do not over-tighten; increase pressure until the bleeding slows to a trickle, and always try to reduce pressure, not increase. Remember to release the tourniquet every ten minutes to allow oxygen to flow to tissues below the wound. After twenty or thirty minutes, try using only a pressure bandage to quell the bleeding. Realize that someone should be driving you to the nearest emergency clinic while this is happening. Make sure to take rags and towels with you to catch any blood that spills. Your friend will not take kindly to having blood all over the upholstery in the car.

One more point; any cat who has an aversion to being handled will not take kindly to all this physical manipulation. You may need to wear long clothing and gloves as a safety precaution. The best thing, of course, is to desensitize the cat to handling from an early age.

The same rules apply for deep punctures. Stopping the bleeding is the most important first step. No puncture wound should go unseen by your vet, owing to the frequency of infections and abscesses. In addition, the injury, normally a bite from another animal, could transmit some viral or bacterial disease that could prove fatal if left untreated.

Car Accidents

No cat should ever be hit by a car, because no cat should ever be allowed outdoors unsupervised. If, as is all too frequently the case, your cat slips out unnoticed and the inevitable does happen, you will probably have a very serious situation on your hands. Here are some steps to take when dealing with this traumatic event: Do not panic. If you witness your cat being struck by a car, your instinctive reaction might be to become hysterical and to act irrationally instead of calmly and methodically. Remember that your cat will need your help more than ever if it does become seriously injured, so stay cool and put your thinking cap on.

Assess the Situation

How badly does the cat seem to be hurt? Is it walking around, or lying on the ground? Conscious or unconscious? Bleeding or not? Do you see evidence of broken bones or compound fractures?

These important assessments are crucial to treatment, and focusing on them will give you something to do to keep from panicking.

Stay with the Cat, and Call Out for Help

Usually the driver of the car will be concerned enough to stick around, especially if you arrive quickly. He or she may even have a cell phone handy for you to call the emergency vet clinic (always keep emergency numbers in your wallet). The driver or a bystander can make the call as well. If the driver took off (barbarian!) and there is no one in sight, yell your head off until someone notices you.

Keep the Cat Still

Do not move a seriously injured cat unless absolutely necessary. There could be spinal cord damage; if this is so, moving the cat could exacerbate the problem and increase the chances of paralysis. To prevent this, keep the injured cat as still as possible. Even a cat that is walking around may have serious internal injuries that can be compounded by excess movement. Be prepared to physically immobilize the cat by holding it if necessary, and realize that you might take some serious licks, including bites and scratches, due to the cat's panic. Do not let the cat run away, whatever you do; it could injure itself further, or disappear for days, returning home only when it is too late for treatment. Gingerly placing the cat in a travel crate or box is the best way to keep it calm and still; covering any openings in the crate or box with a towel will further act as a calming device. If possible, get a neighbor or bystander to go to your home and get the travel crate or box. You may have to trust a total stranger to do this, but in a time of emergency, you are left with little choice. A blanket inside the crate or box will help comfort the cat and keep it warm.

If a container of some sort is not available, you will have to carry the cat to the car or the home. This must be done carefully and slowly. Nestle the cat's head in the crux of your elbow, with its body resting on the inside of your forearm. With your free hand, hold the cat firmly by the nape of its neck, to prevent it from leaping out of your arms. Again, realize that you may be bitten or scratched, try not to let this affect your efforts.

Determine if the Cat Has Serious Injuries

Profuse bleeding, bad breaks, or compound fractures will be clearly evident. Severe bleeding will need to be dealt with (see the sections earlier in this chapter regarding pressure bandaging and tourniquets), but many breaks or fractures will not need to be splinted, if the cat is kept still in a crate or box.

Evaluate if the Cat Has Gone into Shock

An animal is said to be in shock when its tissues are not being adequately supplied with blood and oxygen. Most often caused by a severe drop in blood pressure owing to blood loss from either internal or external bleeding, shock can easily kill a cat if not treated quickly.

Any cat showing signs of shock needs to see a vet as soon as possible; delay could prove fatal. In the interim, keep the cat as warm as possible.

Even if your cat seems fine after the car accident, take it to the vet. Internal injuries do not always make themselves obvious, but can lead to death within a few days.

ANIMAL ATTACKS

Although this is yet another situation that can be minimized by keeping your cat indoors, your feline may still find itself on the wrong end of a bite one day, perhaps from another cat (or dog) in your own home. Whatever the source, your cat could be seriously hurt or killed by an attack from another animal, not only by direct trauma, but by the passing of infectious diseases such as rabies. Bites from insects or snakes can also be injurious or fatal, and should not be taken lightly. Wounds from animal attacks are outlined here.

Puncture Wounds

Puncture wounds should be cleaned and dressed properly, then seen by a vet as soon as possible. Punctures can easily abscess; they should be irrigated well with an antibacterial solution and kept as clean as possible to prevent infection. As with any infectious situation, your vet may want to put your cat on antibiotics for a short period of time. Serious puncture wounds may require suturing. Up-to-date vaccinations will provide crucial protection for a cat if it is attacked by another animal; do not be lax on these.

Serious Cuts, Tears, or Scratches

You can attend to serious cuts or scratches, but these will still require a visit to the vet, as well as treatment with antibiotics, especially if the attacker was another cat (as cats have bacteria-laden mouths and claws). Any scratch of the cornea should be seen by a vet immediately, as it could cause cataracts, eye infections, or blindness.

Broken or Fractured Bones

Sometimes caused by an attack from a large animal, broken or fractured bones need to be treated as soon as possible by your vet. Put the injured cat in a travel crate (after splinting the limbs or tail if appropriate) and head for the emergency cat clinic.

Broken or Missing Teeth

After an animal attack, check your cat's mouth for broken or missing teeth. Any broken tooth in which the root is exposed needs treatment from your vet. If the entire tooth, root and all, is gone, treat the socket with an oral disinfectant (mouthwash, salt water, or 0.05% hydrogen peroxide will work), using a cotton swab. Then get your vet to take a look.

SNAKE AND INSECT BITES

Snake Bites

A bite from a poisonous snake or reptile can often be fatal to your cat. Though rare (few cats hunt these creatures), the occasional unlucky cat does get bitten by a rattlesnake, water moccasin, gila monster, or other venomous reptile.

Unless you discover your cat immediately after a bite from one of these characters, you may be too late. The bite from a mature rattlesnake can kill an adult human, who can weigh fifteen to twenty times as much as a cat. If you witness the attack or get there right away, you should apply a tourniquet several inches above the affected area (unless it is to the face or body), and get to the vet pronto. Remember to loosen the tourniquet every ten minutes, to allow needed oxygen to reach body tissues. If you have a snake-bite kit available, you can use it on your cat while someone drives you to the vet. Treatment involves making small X-incisions over each fang wound with a single-edged razor blade, then applying suction cups to each wound to prevent the venom from slowly seeping into the cat's lymph system. The punctures should also be cleaned with an antibacterial solution when possible.

Be forewarned that no cat will remain calm during any of this, especially when you make the X-incisions. You will probably have a panicked, biting cat to deal with.

Insect Bites

A cat who is attacked and bitten or stung by a venomous insect can sustain pain and swelling but rarely death, unless it suffers a severe allergic reaction to the venom, resulting in what is called "anaphylactic shock," which can lead to death. Insects to be especially concerned about are:

> Bees, wasps, and hornets
> Certain species of ants and spiders
> Scorpions

Only black widow spiders and scorpions are capable of killing a nonallergic cat with their venom, except if the animal is stung by many bees, wasps, or hornets. Treatment for an insect attack involves fast removal of any stingers and a thorough cleaning of the area. The repeated applications of a cool cloth can help minimize swelling and pain. If you see symptoms such as vomiting, disorientation, or shock, see your vet as soon as possible.

POISONING

If your cat has ingested a poisonous plant or another toxic substance, you may need to act quickly to save its life. The most common treatment is to induce vomiting, which removes the toxin from the cat's stomach before it has the chance to get into the system. The exception to this is when the cat has ingested a very corrosive material such as drain cleaner, acid, chlorine powder, antifreeze, tarnish remover, fertilizer, or fuel of any type. Forcing these harsh substances back up will further damage the cat's esophagus and oral cavity.

Vomiting can be induced in a cat by administering two teaspoons of syrup of ipecac, or, if that is not available, two teaspoons of heavily salted water (this is not as effective, and may need to be repeated). After the cat has vomited, give it as much water or milk as you can; force-feed this with a turkey baster if need be. Then get to your vet as soon as possible. Do not attempt to induce vomiting if the cat is losing consciousness or is having seizures.

Other techniques for minimizing the effects of poison can be used, including activated charcoal tablets, which can absorb many poisons and prevent their absorption into the cat's system.

Make sure to have a talk with your vet regarding antidotes and emergency treatment for poisoning in your cat. Remember, keep the lines of communication open. The best method is of course prevention; keep all toxic substances out of your cat's reach! You can also call the National Animal Poison Information Center, twenty-four hours a day, for advice. Their telephone number is 1-800-548-2423. There is a charge for the service. Your local 911 service might also be able to give you some advice, but I advise you to have the telephone number of an emergency cat clinic on hand for times like these.

Choking

A rare occurrence in cats, choking can still occur if a large piece of food or a foreign body becomes firmly lodged in the cat's throat. If your cat is unconscious, you will need to perform artificial respiration and perhaps CPR as well. If the cat is still conscious, however, you should first see if the obstruction can be removed with your fingers, forceps or tweezers. If the object cannot be reached or is not visible, lie the cat on its side, place the heel of your hand just below the last rib (where the diaphragm is located), and give two or three quick pushes, straight down. This is the feline version of the Heimlich maneuver. It should force air up the windpipe and hopefully dislodge or expel the object. As in all emergency situations, get your cat to the vet as soon as possible. Ideally, you should be performing first aid on your cat while in the back seat of a car that is headed for the clinic.

Seizures

Identified by sudden uncontrolled movements of the muscles, seizures in a cat can be caused by any number of factors, including poisoning, injury, and epilepsy. Some cats, according to the cause, might have only one seizure at a time, spaced out over days or even weeks, whereas others can suffer multiple seizures in a very short period.

A cat in a convulsive seizure can be a great danger to itself and to you. The cat doesn't act rationally during this time; it may not even recognize you. The cat may bite or scratch you or anyone who tries to restrain it. If you can predict when the seizure is about to occur, the best course of action is to ether wrap the cat in a blanket or place it in a small travel crate or box to restrict its movement and prevent injury. If you have previous experience with your cat's having seizures and know that it does not become violently aggressive during an episode, then simply restrain the cat in a towel until the seizure is over.

Falls

Cats have the incredible ability to survive falls from great heights, often with little or no injury. Sometimes, though, a cat can suffer internal injuries that go unnoticed by its owner. If your cat takes a fall of more than fifteen or twenty feet, it might be advisable to talk to your vet. If the cat falls from higher than that, you should definitely head for the vet as soon as possible. Take care to move the cat as little as possible, to prevent possible injury to the spinal cord. Hold the cat still in your arms if necessary, or place it in a small, towel-lined travel crate for the trip to the vet. You will not be able to strap the cat to a board of any type; this will panic the cat, possibly causing further injury.

Euthanasia

Though cats of today are living longer and healthier lives than those of just a generation ago, there will come a time when, no matter how accommodating you become, and no matter what wonders your vet works, your cat will simply no longer be able to live comfortably and happily. When the cat's bowel and bladder movements fail, when the appetite is gone, and when the senses no longer function, it should be time for you to sit down with your vet and have a heart-to-heart talk about what your options are. Euthanasia is kind and painless for the old cat, and can release your pet from great humiliation and suffering. Many owners will not consider having their beloved cat put to sleep until it is in dire pain; this is understandable, considering that we rarely if ever use the same rationale regarding those people that we love so very much. Some will argue: why shouldn't our pets have the same consideration? All too often, our views of life and death, for ourselves and our pets, become clouded and desperate when we face the ultimate decision.

A dog or cat can be with us for upward of twenty years. We bond, share emotions and experiences, and make each other feel good. Our pets soothe us; we fall for each other. A pet can often be more forgiving, empathetic, and loyal than many people in our lives. It makes perfect sense that we as loving owners and companions would not want to simply put our pets "to sleep" when their bodies fail them.

The impending loss of a loving companion, regardless of species, is a painful experience, but should not be avoided simply to save yourself pain. Always remember that an old cat in failing health can often be in great pain that sometimes cannot be eased. The cat whose kidneys completely fail, for instance, has little recourse. An old cat with debilitating arthritis throughout its body cannot be relieved of that all-encompassing pain; to allow it to linger on simply because we might not be able to deal with the loss is selfish and cruel.

A single owner who has never been emotionally invested in a family with children may be devastated by the thought of having his or her old feline friend put to sleep. It has been sibling, child, friend, and in some cases a substitute mate; the death of such a cat means isolation and great feelings of loss for this person, who may easily lose sight of the fact that the cat is being asked to tolerate great pain and discomfort as a means of postponing human grief.

Though the option of euthanasia can sometimes be abused (or made necessary by the folly of owners who carelessly allow their cats to breed and produce kittens with nowhere to go), it is more often considered too late.

Deciding whether or not to peacefully end the life of a cat who is suffering incurable cancer or irreversible organ damage or is in great pain with no hope of relief is a choice best made by all the family members. Even young children should at least be informed of the situation, using your best intuitive parenting skills. If one member of the family is vehemently against the possibility of euthanizing the cat, you may all need to discuss the situation with your vet, who will help put things into better medical perspective.

He or she will give you all a candid prognosis, and will tell you just exactly what all your options are.

All options should be carefully considered, however. Sometimes a diagnosis of a terminal illness is inaccurate, and sometimes a novel combination of therapies and techniques can relieve a cat's pain and improve its quality of life immensely. Be sure to cover all the bases, including getting a second opinion on any devastating diagnosis. Realize that your vet is in business to save lives, not take them; most would never opt to euthanize when any viable alternatives are available.

Once the decision to euthanize is made, your vet will explain the procedure to you. Done by the intravenous injection of an overdose of a type of anesthetic, death comes rapidly and peacefully, without pain or discomfort.

Heading serious feline illnesses off at the pass involves keen observational skills on your part. In addition to the aforementioned symptoms of impending illness and obvious behavioral changes, there are other symptoms that you as an owner should pay attention to and report to your vet, allowing him or her to judge whether a trip to the clinic is necessary. They include:

- A temperature of 103 to 105 degrees Fahrenheit
- Any evidence of diarrhea or vomiting in combination with a fever or other signs of illness
- Severe dehydration, which can be diagnosed by lifting and releasing a pinch of skin on the cat's back, and watching to see how quickly it rebounds. If it takes more than a moment, your cat may be dehydrated.
- Persistent lethargy combined with poor appetite and weight loss
- Bad breath combined with excessive thirst

- A cough or wheeze accompanied by fever
- Runny nose or eyes, with a cough or fever
- Persistent limping or obvious pain in the limbs or spinal column
- Persistent vomiting, especially with fever or diarrhea
- Any lumps or swollen areas that seem painful and warm or are discharging pus or blood
- Pale gums and lethargy, possibly combined with loss of appetite or fever

Symptoms that warrant an immediate trip to the vet include:

- A fever of over 105 degrees Fahrenheit, whether any other symptoms are present or not
- Any type of paralysis, be it partial or complete
- A fever of over 103 degrees Fahrenheit that is accompanied by severe shortness of breath, extreme lethargy, and lack of appetite
- Any signs that your cat may have consumed any type of toxic substances, including difficulty breathing, excessive lethargy, vomiting, or diarrhea
- Any type of wound that won't stop bleeding
- An infected abscess accompanied by persistent high fever
- Any serious trauma from an attack by another animal or person
- Any cessation of breathing or consciousness
- Any broken limbs or trauma to the eye
- Persistent bloody diarrhea or vomit

In addition, there are more subtle signs of illness to be aware of, such as a reduced (but not absent) appetite, intermittent signs of lameness, sudden changes in sleeping patterns, excessive (or nonexistent) grooming, excessive vocalization, or increased irritability in an otherwise happy, friendly cat.

You are the best judge of your cat's moods, habits, and general state of mind. If you know your cat, you will be able to pick up on very subtle little changes that no one else could. If you have children, you know what I'm talking about; their teacher will never notice changes that are painfully obvious to you and your spouse. That's how a cat owner "in tune" with his or her cat is. Trust your gut feelings, and, when in doubt, see your vet. The worst that can happen is you'll be out forty or fifty dollars in exchange for a little peace of mind.

CHAPTER 10

Health Care for Cats

What's Up, Pussycat?

As with humans, early diagnosis of any illness is crucial to a feline's survival. Whether it be a urinary tract infection, arthritis, diabetes, or a more serious illness like cancer, knowing what to look for and consulting your veterinarian is paramount. It's equally important that you familiarize yourself with the latest veterinary accomplishments so that you and kitty are prepared for any medical situations that may arise.

Decades of research and hard science have led to unbelievable advancement in medicine and technology, and those beneficial discoveries and procedures apply not to only to humans, but to animals as well. Feline diseases that in the past might have been fatal, such as diabetes or thyroid conditions, are now very treatable. Veterinary advancements have also made it possible for cats infected with serious illnesses, such as feline immunodeficiency virus (FIV) and feline leukemia virus (FeLV), to live for many years if their diagnosis is made early.

Significant growth in the feral cat population has unfortunately led to an increase in the spread of disease, and as such, has contributed to several growing trends in feline health care, including more advanced local veterinary care, feline disease specialists, pet medical insurance, and healthier feline cuisine. These advancements have all been a great benefit to the feline population.

A growing number of veterinarians provide exceptional in-office care for cats diagnosed with diabetes, allergies, and thyroid conditions that in the past may have required the services of specialists. Many treatments are available that are noninvasive, with prescribed medications and monitored diet plans.

That's not to say that the number of specialists has diminished. In fact, the number of practicing veterinary specialists is on the rise, as more and more owners are now taking their cats to specialists when their feline is faced with a long-term disability or life-threatening illness. As a result, there are many options for cats suffering from cancer or various bone-related afflictions.

As the human patient population is well aware, specialists can be expensive. Fortunately for pet owners there is a solution to this problem in the form of pet insurance. A quick Internet search will show you that there are a wide variety of medical insurance policies available for your pets. In most cases, these policies can be tailored to your needs, and can include everything from veterinary fees to accident coverage, and even death benefits.

Yet another aspect of veterinary care that has proven to be a healthy benefit to the feline community is the availability of prescribed well-rounded and specialized cat foods created for both healthy cats and those with specific needs, such as age, obesity, diabetes, or liver and kidney problems. These foods and their host of healthy ingredients are making a huge impact on a feline population that in many ways suffers afflictions similar to those of overindulging humans.

Veterinary advancement is a good thing for kitty, but the only way your cat can benefit from good medicine is for you to be informed of current problems, treatments, and maintenance programs available for your cat.

Local Treatment

If you already own a cat and have been to the vet then you've probably noticed that your vet has a wide range of treatments and inner-office procedures available. In the past, more serious ailments that affect felines such as thyroid disorders may have required the services of a specialist. That has changed. Nowadays, cats diagnosed with diabetes, urinary problems, arthritis, or kidney or liver afflictions can receive excellent treatment at their vet's office.

Even thyroid issues like hyperthyroidism (where the thyroid gland is overactive) and hypothyroidism (where the gland is underactive), can be treated locally with prescribed medication. When you might find need of a specialist, in this case, is if your cat requires radioactive iodine treatment. Regardless of the situation, your vet will outline a treatment for your cat and offer all possible solutions.

Always remember that your vet is your best source of information when it comes to all things feline. Don't ever hesitate to ask your vet if you think your cat is having a problem, or if you're unclear about a procedure or treatment.

RUNNING WILD: FATAL ATTRACTION

When it comes to feline afflictions—whether they be minor ailments or life threatening diseases—there are plenty. As with humans, the main spread of disease can be controlled, but it's a matter of uncovering and stabilizing the sources of diseases, and that's not easy if you have an uncooperative or complacent human population.

Feral animals, by definition, are wild beasts; those not domesticated, cultivated, or who have escaped domestication. As the human population increases, so does the population of feral cats and the spread of the two most virulent and fatal feline diseases: feline immunodeficiency virus (FIV) and feline leukemia virus (FeLV). Both are retroviruses (such as the HIV virus in humans) that humans and dogs cannot contract through contact—they strictly affect cats.

Most cats acquire FIV through bites or scratches when they fight with an infected cat, which is why outdoor cats are more susceptible to the disease. The FeLV disease is spread through contact with saliva, urine, or blood.

Feral cats are often carriers of these and other diseases, being that they lack regular medical care. Owners who allow their cats to run wild without giving them immunizations, or who refuse to have their cats spayed or neutered, contribute to this growing problem. In the case of FeLV, infected felines can pass the disease on to their young, who can then continue to pass it on if they're not spayed or neutered.

There are many symptoms of these two killer diseases, so the best thing you can do is take your animal to the vet to ascertain exactly what the problem is. If your cat spends unsupervised time outdoors and has not been regularly vaccinated, your cat runs a higher risk of exposure, as their free roaming capacity enables them to come into contact with feral cats. At present, there are no vaccinations for FIV and there is no cure for either disease, so it's very important to consult your vet about methods of prevention.

According to *www.healthypet.com*, there are several preventative measures you can take to keep your cat safe:

"Make sure your cat is never exposed to an FIV-positive or FeLV-positive cat. This means keeping your cat indoors and separated from all cats of unknown FeLV and FIV status. Unsupervised outdoor activity puts cats at risk. There is no way to ensure that cats allowed to roam freely outdoors will not be exposed to other cats that have an immune deficiency disease. Most cats currently infected with FIV or FeLV were first exposed to the disease through this kind of contact."

It's very important to have all of your cats tested for FIV and FeLV on a regular basis. In particular, testing is recommended for:

- Any newly acquired kitten or adult cat before it joins a multiple-cat household and prior to the first FeLV vaccine.
- Any cat used for breeding.
- Any cat with known FIV or FeLV exposure (if the first test is negative, retest every three to six months for one year).
- Any sick cat with symptoms that suggest FIV or FeLV infection.

Recognizing the Signs

Cats infected with FIV or FeLV can survive for a number of years if the illness is detected in its early stages. Having your cat regularly tested not only increases the chances of your cat living a long and healthy life, but it helps prevent the spread of disease if your cat is indeed infected. A simple blood test is usually all that's required to diagnose FIV or FeLV and most veterinarians can provide in-house results quickly.

The American Association of Feline Practitioners (AAFP), an organization of vets focused on maintaining cat health care, lists the following criteria you should know about to help determine when to have your cat tested. FIV and FeLV testing is important in the following situations:

- If your cat has never been tested before.
- If your cat is sick, even if it may have tested free of infection in the past.
- When cats are newly adopted, whether or not they will be entering a household with other cats.
- If your cat has recently been exposed to an infected cat.
- If your cat is exposed to cats that may be infected (for example, if your cat goes outdoors unsupervised, or lives with other cats that might be infected). Your veterinarian may suggest testing periodically as long as your cat is potentially exposed to infected cats.
- Prior to your cat receiving an FeLV vaccine (in this case, FeLV testing is the most important).

On their Web site, the AAFP provides a feline observation form that you can fill out prior to visiting your vet (*www.fivtest.com/gethelp/index.cfm*), which will help narrow down particular symptoms your cat may be experiencing, and help the vet test your cat accordingly.

Some of the signs to watch out for are a marked decrease in appetite or grooming, weakness or lethargy, and a host of more serious side effects that require immediate attention. As rule, whenever you notice behaviors that are not normal for your cat, you should always consult your vet immediately. Your vet is your best source of information, and the one person who is intimately aware of your cat's history and physiology.

When to Visit a Specialist

The prominence of long-term illness in the feline community has resulted in an increase in the number of vets specializing in particular diseases. In the past, an owner might have put a cat to sleep if it was diagnosed with a terminal illness such as cancer. These days, owners are more apt to take their cat to a feline cancer specialist. The same holds true for cats suffering from arthritis, bone disorders, bone breaks, and fractures. Owners are now making use of feline osteopaths and orthopedic specialists.

If your cat can benefit from the service of a specialist, your vet will be able to direct you to an appropriate local source. Having an ill cat is never easy, but your vet is innately in tune to the relationship between you and your cat. In the end, both you and your vet want to select a treatment that's most beneficial to your cat.

FANCY FEASTING

A particular commonality that all creatures great and small have is a propensity for overeating and obesity. Whether you're a human, dog, or feline, you run the risk of packing on pounds, no matter if your vice is a cheeseburger, Alpo, or Meow Mix. The past few years have shown a definite increase in numbers of overweight felines, and diseases associated with obesity such as diabetes and arthritis.

Food manufacturers have taken this to heart by producing various foods geared toward helping your cat maintain a healthy lifestyle without sacrificing the need to feed. Diabetes, obesity, and urinary tract infections are the most common food-related afflictions cats face. Fortunately, with the creation of a vast number of specialty foods, these problems can be more readily controlled.

It's very important that owners read the labels of their cat's food to determine that it contains all of the necessary nutrients appropriate for their cat's size and age. Kittens obviously require foods higher in protein and fat, while more mature or senior cats require less calories due to increased inactivity.

It's important to consult your vet about the type of food that is best for your cat during its various stages of growth. Some cats, for example, may require higher percentages of ash or magnesium, while others may have trouble digesting various byproducts. Taurine is a crucial element to all cat foods; one that helps keep a cat's heart healthy and their vision clear. It's also important to be on the lookout for foods that contain chicken or meat byproducts (such as ground chicken beaks) or foods overloaded with grains such as corn.

Once you find a food that contains all of the necessary nutrients your cat requires—and one you can get them to eat—feeding time becomes an issue of simple maintenance. Indoor cats who don't experience the same level of exercise as an outdoor cat are particularly susceptible to obesity. Cats who have been spayed or neutered also don't require as much sustenance. Bear in mind that a cat is like a goldfish—if you overfeed it, it'll balloon! You need to take special care to monitor the amount of food your cat consumes and adjust their intake accordingly if they gain or lose too much weight.

It's crucial to consult your vet before starting your cat on a particular feeding program, especially if your cat suffers from diabetes or urinary tract problems. Your vet will be able to put your cat on a diet that is safe and will provide consistent maintenance for their body type and digestive capabilities

Insuring Your Pet

For most pet owners, veterinary services translate to yearly checkups, shots, and occasional extra visits for minor problems that arise. But what happens when your cat is faced with a disability or life-threatening illness? Like humans, the cost for vets who specialize in serious afflictions such as thyroid conditions or cancers can be high. In response to that growing need, companies are now offering pet insurance. You can insure Fluffy just as you would any other family member.

Information on pet insurance is readily available on the Internet. As with humans, policies vary, so do your homework and read the fine print. Policies can cover everything from veterinary fees, accidents, boarding fees, theft and reward fees if your pet strays or is stolen, and even holiday and death benefits. It may sound amazing, but in reality, it could be a handy thing to have when tragedy strikes. After all, you have health insurance for yourself, why not for the cat?

To Claw or Not to Claw

The subject of declawing a cat is highly controversial, but it must be mentioned if for no other reason than many cat owners don't fully understand the process and its implications. There are many reasons why people choose to have their cat declawed, be it that Fluffy is decimating the furniture, or that there's a concern that children may be scratched. Regardless of the reason, it's important that you understand what declawing involves and that you explore all other options before having the procedure performed.

Declawing a cat is a common practice in the United States, but in many countries it is outlawed. The common misconception is that a cat's claws are simply removed, much like a human fingernail; but that is not the case. Declawing is an irreversible process that involves multiple amputations. Basically, you'd be removing the last part of your cat's toes. The declawing surgery removes bones, ligaments, tendons, and nerves that help a cat's body stay in balance. (If comparing it to a human's anatomy it's akin to amputating a human's fingertips at the first knuckle.) That said, you can see why declawing can be painful for your cat, can cause long-term emotional and physical trauma, and can inhibit most of the pleasures a cat enjoys, including walking, running, stretching, and playing.

It must also be said that that like humans, cats react to pain and the declawing procedure in different ways. Some cats may show few or no side effects of the surgery, while others endure a higher level of trauma. Before you consider a declawing procedure, you need to be well informed, and that means consulting with your vet about the procedure and exploring all other possible options. Many experts feel that bad scratching behaviors are 100 percent correctable, so before you decide to declaw, you should make sure every other option is completely exhausted.

Scratch and Sniff

So what can you do to prevent Fluffy from becoming a feline Freddy Krueger? First, know that scratching is instinctive for cats—it's what they do—and no amount of scolding is going to save the sofa. All cats scratch something, so the goal is to have them scratch something that isn't valuable. A winning situation is for you to find a solution that will work for both you and Fluffy, whether it be a cat condo she can decimate, a sisel rope scratching post, or her own area rug. Cats love rough surfaces, so give her a good substitute that she can claim, and chances are she'll steer clear of the pristine recliner or chair legs.

Keep in mind that training a cat to scratch only certain items when they're still kittens is half the battle. Adult cats can be set in their ways, but it's not impossible to change their behavior with various catnip enticements, or a scratching post or cat condo in a communal family room. Whatever you decide to try, make sure that it's stable and tall enough for kitty to completely stretch. If your cat seems disinterested in a scratching post, try spraying it with a catnip solution or simply sprinkling a little catnip all over it. Chances are, it'll be too good for Fluffy to pass up.

Felines mark their territory and various items with pheromones strategically located on their body. If your cat is consumed by a certain spot or item and continues to scratch, it's because it has left a scent marker. If you need to discourage kitty from returning to a favorite decimation spot, try citrus sprays. Cats have a natural aversion to citrus, and lemon- or orange-scented sprays may make an area less enticing to a cat, especially if there's catnip to be found elsewhere. Your ultimate goal is to make Fluffy's destruction zone unattractive. If citrus proves futile, there are a host of other products available, such as pheromone sprays that could make your cat turn tail. Also, you might try double-sided tape or aluminum foil. Items that are no fun to scratch won't hold kitty's interest for long.

One of the newest alternatives to declawing are nail caps which are glued onto your cat's claws. Manufacturers like Soft Paws (*www.softpaws.com*) provide this humane alternative and it is fast catching on. Suitable for both indoor and outdoor cats, these vinyl caps fit snugly over Fluffy's claws, thereby eliminating the shred factor.

The Internet is a wonderful source of information when it comes to all things feline. Organizations like Cats International (*www.catsinternational.org*), the Humane Society of the United States (*www.hsus.org*), and CatScratching.com (*www.catscratching.com*) are great places to find information relating to cat behaviors and the options you have when it comes to preventing bad behaviors.

Before you declaw, explore all options:

- Consult your vet in order to thoroughly understand the declawing procedure and other alternatives.
- Know that cats will scratch no matter what, and punishment won't have an impact.
- Trim your cat's nails.
- Make your cat's decimation area unattractive by using citrus, pheromone spray, double-sided tape or aluminum foil.
- Get kitty a scratching post with a rough surface like carpet, corregated cardboard, or sisel rope.
- Sprinkle the acceptable scratching post or cat condo with catnip or other enticements.
- Reinforce kitty's good behavior by petting her when she scratches the correct object.
- If citrus or tape doesn't deter kitty, try using a whistle or spray water bottle when kitty scratches inappropriate items or areas.
- Consider using nail caps on kitty's claws as an alternative to declawing.

Play It Smart

For most individuals, cats are akin to children. They are loyal and loving companions who bring joy and comfort to owners the world over. Much as you would care for a child, you should also care for your cat, and that means being constantly aware of how your cat is feeling.

Cats become ill for myriad reasons. They might simply catch a cold or contract a curable infection. The difference between felines and children is that Fluffy can't tell you exactly how she's feeling, so it's up to you to pay attention and watch for signs of distress. There is a wide variety of symptoms to watch out for:

- Is your cat losing or gaining weight?
- Does he refuse to eat or appear ravenous?
- Does he appear lethargic, or is he having trouble breathing?
- Does he have a half-eyed expression rather than clear wide-open eyes?
- Is his sleep pattern interrupted?
- Is he irritable or exhibiting uncommon behavior?
- Is he being reclusive or retreating from family members or other household cats?
- Does he suddenly not enjoy being petted?
- Are his whiskers pulled back toward their face? (Happy cats have extended whiskers.)
- Is he neglecting his grooming? Is his fur coarse or ragged?
- Is he constantly scratching or repeatedly sneezing?
- Are his bowel movements consistent?
- Is he having trouble urinating? Is the problem excessive urination or lack of typical urination?

Any of these symptoms in some form or another should be a cue that you need to get your cat to the vet. In most cases, the solution may be nothing more than antibiotics, or perhaps a change in diet. Regardless, it's not worth taking the risk that something more serious is affecting your cat. Under no circumstances should you take the risk of diagnosing your own cat. If you notice any of the above symptoms, get Fluffy into the carrier and see your vet immediately.

Happily Ever After

Whether it be specialization, insurance, cuisine, controlling a feral population, or the controversial declawing process, you can bet that individuals in the veterinary field have their hands full. Fortunately, continuous medical advancements are giving vets and owners the tools they need to help cats live long and happy lives.

Index

A

Age of cat
    cat choice and, 20–21
    food and, 69–73, 91, 93
    older cats and, 89–94
Aggression, 8, 114–116
Agility tournaments, 130–131
American Association of Feline Practitioners (AAFP), 174
American Bobtail breed, 127
American Curl breed, 126–127
Attacks, by other animals, 158–160
Aversion therapy, 104–105

B

Beds, 42
Behavior
    of cats versus dogs, 10–12
    changes in, 146–147
    of strays, 19–20
    temperament and, 17, 19–20
    see also Body language; Problem behaviors
Bites, 160–161
Biting, 49, 115–116
Bleeding, first aid for, 153–156
Body language, 133–138, 140–144
Bombay breed, 127–128
Breeders, 83–84, 129–130
Breeding, 18
Breed types
    purebred cats, 14–18, 32
    types of, 126–129
Brushing, 44, 75–76

C

Canned food, 70
Car accidents, first aid after, 156–158
Cat Fanciers' Association (CFA) International Cat Show, 120–121
Children, introducing new cat to, 48
Choking, 162–163
Choosing a cat, 13–32
    advantages over dogs, 3–12
    age issues, 20–21
    behavior/temperament issues, 17, 19–20
    breed rescues and, 129–130
    cost issues, 15–16
    health issues, 17–18, 19
    purebred versus mixed breed, 14–18, 32
Citrus sprays, 179
Claws
    cat shows and, 123–124
    shields for, 111
    trimming of, 45, 76–78
    see also Scratching
Clicker, 63
Coat care, 75–76

183

Collar, 46–47
Comb, 44
"Come," teaching cat to, 62–63
Communication, see Body language; Vocalization
Conditioned responses, 61–62
Constipation, 73
Costs, of acquiring cat, 15–16
Crate, 43–44, 57–58, 123, 124
Crying, 50
Cuts and scrapes, 153–154, 159

D

Declawing, 177–180
Diet, see Food
Dishes, for food and water, 40, 123, 124
Dogs
    cats contrasted to, 3–12
    introducing new cat to, 49–50, 61
    litter box location and, 55
    safety and, 87–88
Domestication, 8–9, 96
Dominant cat behavior, 104–105

E

Ears, 78–79, 137–138
Egyptian Mau breed, 128
Euthanasia, 15, 164–168
Exercise, 7, 88
Eyes, 140–141

F

Falls, first aid for, 163–164
Fecal sample, 85
Feline immunodeficiency virus (FIV), 172–174
Feline leukemia virus (FeLV), 172–174
Feral cats, disease and, 170, 171–175

First aid, 151–152
    after animal attacks, 158–160
    after car accidents, 156–158
    for bites, 160–161
    for choking, 162–163
    for cuts and scrapes, 153–154
    for falls, 163–164
    first-aid kit, 45–46
    for fractures and breaks, 154–156
    for poisoning, 161–162
    for seizures, 163
    taking temperature and pulse, 152
Food, 40–41
    age of cat and, 69–73, 91, 93
    finicky eating and, 112–114
    free feeding versus scheduled feeding, 62, 73–75, 112
    overfeeding and, 72
    specialty, 170–171, 175–176
Fractures and breaks, 154–156, 159
Free-feeding, 62, 73–75, 112

G

Grooming, 8
    of aging cat, 94
    coat care, 75–76
    ear cleaning, 78–79
    nail trimming, 76–78
    supplies for, 44–45
    teeth and gum care, 79–80
Gums, care of, 79–80

H

Hairless cats, 128
Harness, 47, 64–67
Health issues
    aging and, 89–94
    cat choice and, 17–18
    declawing, 177–180

exercise and, 88
failure to use litter box, 97–100
feral cats and disease, 170, 171–175
importance of early diagnosis of illness, 169–170
of indoor versus outdoor cat, 36–37
medical advancements and, 169–171, 175
overfeeding, 72
record-keeping and, 88–89
signs of illness, 141, 166–168, 180–182
of strays, 19
see also First aid; Veterinarians
Hissing, 139
Home environment
introducing cat to, 48–51
preparing for cat, 38–40, 47–48, 86–88
Horner, Nikki, 127–128
Housebreaking, 6, 7
House-soiling problems, see Litter box; Spraying
Humane Society shelters, 20–21
Hunting for prey, 147–148

I

Identification, 46–47
Indoor cat, 36–38, 92–93
Insurance, 170, 177
International Cat Agility Tournaments (ICAT), 130–131

K

Kneading, 143

L

Leash, 47, 64–67
Legs, body language and, 142–143

Litter, 41–42, 98–99
Litter box, 41
aging cat and, 94
for cat shows, 123, 124
failure to use, 97–100
showing new cat location of, 51, 54
training to use, 54–56
see also Spraying

M

Manx breed, 126–127
Moving, behavior problems and, 100–102, 107–108
Multiple cats, 41, 113, 145–146

N

Nails, see Claws
Name recognition, 56–57
Nervous cat, 107
Neutering, 15, 16, 38, 104–109

O

Outdoor cat
aging and, 92–93
decision about indoor or outdoor, 36–38
hunting by, 147–148
who spray indoors, 105–106

P

Pets (other), 48–50, 60–61, 146. See also Dogs
Poisoning, 161–162
Problem behaviors, 95–116
after family move, 100–102
with litter box use, 97–100
poor eating habits, 112–114
scratching, 42, 109–111, 115–116, 178–180

Problem behaviors, continued
  spraying, 97, 104–109
  with vacations, 102–103
Pulse, how to take, 152
Purring, 139

R

Record-keeping, 88–89
Rescue cats, 129–130
Routine
  changes in aging cat's, 92–94
  establishing for new cat, 51–52
Rubbing, 141–142, 144

S

Scat Mat, 111
Scent glands, 141, 144, 179
Scratching, 42, 109–111, 115–116, 178–180. See also Declawing
Seizures, 163
Shampoo, 45
Shelters, 14–15, 20–21, 83–84
Show cats, 14–18, 32, 119–131
Snake bites, 160–161
Socialization, 58–61
Sphynx, 128
Spraying, 97, 104–109
Stray cats, 18–20, 87
Supplies and equipment, 40–47

T

Tail, body language and, 136–137
Tail-less cats, 126–127
Teeth, 79–80, 160
Temperament, of cat, see Behavior
Temperature, of cat, 92–93, 152
Territorial dominance, 143–146
Toys, 43, 124
Training, 7, 53–67
  to be in crate, 57–58
  to be socialized, 58–61
  to come, 62–63
  feeding and, 62, 73–75
  to have conditioned responses, 61–62
  to recognize name, 56–57
  to use litter box, 54–56
  to walk on leash, 64–67
Travel, avoiding with cat, 102–103
Travel crate, see Crate

U

Urination, to mark territory, 145–146. See also Litter box; Spraying

V

Vacations, behavior problems and, 102–103
Vaccinations, 85, 122, 124
Veterinarians
  American Association of Feline Practitioners (AAFP), 174
  annual checkup with, 84–86
  choosing of, 81–84
  medical advancements and, 169–171, 175
  signs of need for trip to, 167
Vocalization, 138–139
Vomiting, inducing, 162

W

Walking harness, 47, 64–67
Weight, 71–73, 89. See also Food